Two Brothers,
One War

Told by Nancy Bartolotta Fuentes

NFB

<<<>>>

Buffalo, NY

Fuentes, Nancy

Two Brothers, One War: As Told Through the Letters of Edward and Roam Bartz/ Fuentes- 1st Edition

ISBN: 978-0-692477-2-5-0

1.Two Brothers, One War 2.Edward Bartz Roman Bartz 3. Nonfiction.
4.World War II 5. Buffalo, NY
6. No Frills.

NFB
No Frills Buffalo/Amelia Press
119 Dorchester Road
Buffalo, NY 14213

For more information
Please visit
Nofrillsbuffalo.com

Author's Note
These letters are from two brothers to their mother who resided in Buffalo, New York. They were recently discovered and are being shared for purely entertainment purposes. Please excuse any grammatical or spelling errors, as I transcribed them as written. Thank you.

Dedication
This book is dedicated to my husband, Jose L. Fuentes, for finding the letters and supporting me through its completion.

Preface

2013

My husband and I enjoy going to estate and garage sales. One day, during the summer of 2012, my husband came across a box of old letters at one such garage sale. He bought them for $5.00 and brought them home for me to use in my making of greeting cards.

While looking through the envelopes, I realized that they were all addressed to the same person, Mrs. J. Bartz. Upon further investigation, I realized that they were all postmarked between 1940 and 1946.

Since these envelopes were all addressed to the same person, it made me curious as to why she would have saved these letters. What made them so important, so much more important than the ones she hadn't saved?

I came to determine that the majority of the nearly 200 letters were written by her two sons, Edward and Roman. Edward had joined the Army at age 27 and Roman, the Navy at age 22. After reading some of the letters, I felt obligated to transcribe them into a more permanent medium, so as to be able to share this story of a woman and her two sons and just a small part of their lives.

You see, I have since found Edward is still with us, at this writing, at the age of 99 years young and very much looking forward to celebrating his 100th birthday next year. Since he still lives very close to the City of Buffalo, I went to visit him and ask for his permission to continue what I had already started doing. He has given me that permission.

During our conversation, I was pleasantly surprised to realize that Edward, after serving his time in the Army, had returned to employment with the Corps. of Engineers. He later took a position in Personnel at the V. A. Hospital in Buffalo, from which he retired in 1979. It just so happened, that I returned to work after having my children, and took a position
at the V. A. Hospital in Buffalo in 1981. I have since retired as well.

I have returned the box of letters to Edward, since I feel they rightfully belonged to him and only came to me so that I would be the one to share his and his brother's story. I hope in reading this, that you will enjoy the letters as much as I have.

Thank you for your service to our country - Edward and Roman Bartz!

Two Brothers, One War

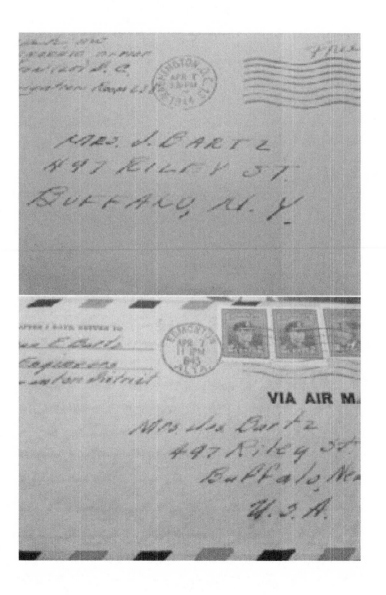

21 September 1940
0900

Dear Mother –

Haven't written in sometime now. Received your letter earlier this week.

There isn't anything worthwhile to do around this office these days. It is all very monotonous and tiring.

Had a letter from Ed about a week ago. Looks like he may be out by the 1st of the year the way things are going.

Have been working almost every evening during the past month. Went to the racetrack last Saturday with the girlfriend. Had a pretty good time.

The weather around here has been cold and rainy lately. Soon we will put our blues on again.

Incidentally I have been 2nd class since August 15.

There really isn't much more to say.

Love

Rum

Detroit, Michigan
October 5th, 1940
11:30 PM

Dear Mother:

It's warm and noisy, too disturbing to sleep right now. There's a football game at the stadium and the crowd and loudspeaker create a lot of noise.

I went to the football game last night and later to a roller skating party. Today I went with another fellow to the ball park where the World Series is being held. We got there 3 hours before game time and all the gates were closed already. In order to get in you would have to wait for over 10 hours. I guess I won't see any World Series this year.

We walked downtown from the stadium and went to the show.

I sent my wash this morning so it should show up about the same time this letter does. I don't think those laundry cases come any longer.

I finished school yesterday. I went to the coordinator's office (the guy who gets the jobs) three times this week. They had several jobs but they required experience. He said however that they are expecting a drafting position from an electric company. If it does come in, I'll be fairly sure of getting it. I hope that it does.

I hadn't had much time to write any letters all week because of the exams which are given at the end of each month. They kept me fairly busy.

There isn't much more to write about – nothing much ever happens...

Love,

Rum

Wednesday, Oct. 9, 1940

Dear Mother:

I received your letter this afternoon. I'm answering it immediately because you wanted to know about the laundry. I have enough of everything except socks but they'll hold out for a week, so you needn't bother about it.

I didn't get any job. I went down yesterday and he said there were a lot of positions but when he looked up my record and saw that I didn't have any industrial experience he said he couldn't do anything for me right now.

It's no use going to school because its just a repetition of what I have had. I have a lot of work however which will be due next month.

What kind of fireman does Ed want to be, a city one or one that shovels coal into a furnace?

If you see Sammy's mother ask her what his address is. I sent him a letter long time ago and never got an answer so I think he never received it.

Does anybody ever take Duchess out for a walk or does she just stay in the house all the while. I wish that I could see her...

You had better take off Saturday and go to Bradford regardless of whether you have to work or not.

I suppose Ed will be the first to be conscripted. They'll give him an office job in the Army because of his heart.

Thanks for the 2 dollars but don't send anymore, I have enough to last me for awhile.

Love,

Rum

Friday, December 13, 1940
Detroit, Michigan

Dear Mother:

I haven't written a letter in a long time but that's because I haven't received any myself. Adeline sent me a letter yesterday. How come that Eds home again I thought he was working in Messana?

I go to work at five o'clock today. I'm coming home for Christmas, in fact I may get home a day or two before Christmas.

It got cold again today and yesterday it rained all day.

The place I work at is at Grand River and Oakman Boulevard. It's about 5 miles from where I'm staying.

That's about all for now.

Love

Rum

May 16, 1941

Dear Mother:

I haven't written in some time because there isn't much to say and besides Ed probably tells you most everything that happens around here. My handwriting is sort of poor because I don't do much writing.

I hope to be home for Decoration Day altho I still don't know whether I will be able to go. It's been warmer then heck here in Massena. Upstairs in the drafting rooms it was 90 (degrees) F. Downstairs it is much cooler.

In case this project folds up I may be transferred elsewhere so I don't have to worry about that.

I just came back from playing tennis.

My wristwatch is somewheres on my dresser and the stem is broken off. I wonder if you could take it to the jeweler and have it fixed. If the charge is more then $2.00 don't bother about it.

I bought a pair of slacks for $6.00 and also a pair of shoes. If I get home, I'll buy a suit because I don't have any clothes at all. My brown pair of trousers I bought last fall are all worn out.

I got a learner's permit now and hope to get a driver's license in the near future if Ed lets me drive the car once in a while and practice up.

That's about all. There's ten bucks enclosed.

Love

Rum

PS1 Show Duchess that snapshot of the Newfoundland dog and myself. The dog is taller then me if it stood up straight.
PS2 Thanks for the shirts, ties, socks and cigarettes!

Thursday – 10:00 PM
August 21, 1941

Dear Mother:

Just dropping you a few short lines. Received your letter on Monday. I sent my laundry out this morning. We just got finished playing ball about an hour and a half ago. It was a very important game as we had to win in order to stay in the playoffs for the Massena Championship. Well, we were losing by the score 10 to 2 in the last inning and then we opened up and scored 9 runs to win 11-10. I was congratulated on playing a very good game and got a hit in the last inning and scored a run. I did sprain my ankle though and its swollen quite a bit so I guess I'll go home and see what I can do for it, as we play again tomorrow and if we win we will meet the Coca Cola team next week, to play 2 out of 3 games for the Massena Championship. So I guess I'll go right home and get some sleep.

Even if you can't come to Massena with Freeman why don't you come down alone anyway? Rum could stay with me and you could have his room, or the other way around; or else you could stay at a tourist home. There are a few of them right on Clark Street. Let me know what you think about it. I think the rest and fresh air would do you lots of good, in addition to the change of scenery. If we had time we could go to Montreal or Lake Placid, or both.

No, I don't think I'll come for Labor Day as it is too long a ride, 600 miles, within 3 days, especially if the car isn't new. I had hoped to take a couple of days off when Lillian graduates at the hospital, which will be on September 9th, but that happens to be just when we are very busy every month, between the 1st and the 10th of the month, so I guess I won't be able to make it. Well, I guess that's about all and I'll mail this right out so that you'll get it on Saturday. S'long.

Love

Ed
PS: I'm enclosing $5.00.

LABOR DAY MORNING
9:55 o'clock
September 1, 1941

Dear Mother:

Well, if this wasn't Labor Day I'd be working rite now, but as it is I came down brite and early to get out a couple of letters.

Did Rum get home alright on Saturday AM?

Well, they finally decided that we won that game which was called off on account of darkness, so tomorrow nite we start playing against the Coca Cola team for the championship of Massena. The team winning 2 out of 3 games is the champion. We received bronze medals on Saturday for being the runners-up in the St. Lawrence Valley Tournament which was held about a month ago. So now if we win the Massena Championship, we get medals and a trophy. We get the medals anyway as we'll be runners-up again in this series.

I wrote letters to Bob Pawlowski and also Henry K., last week and I'm expecting to get an answer this week from them.

It rained all the while from 1 PM on yesterday so didn't do too much. It seems like it will be a grand day today so I might go canoeing and maybe swimming for the last time in this year of 1941.

I guess I still am not sure as to when your vacation is to be; I mean I dunno as to whether its this week and the next, or the next and the week after that. Well, anyway, I'm trying to get the first part of next week off, so that I'll be able to come to Lillian's graduation next Tuesday, September 9th. So I've been just wondering - - if I don't get off I'd probably come next Saturday or Sunday and leave on Wednesday and you could come back with me, instead of coming back with Rum on the train. I'll let you know definitely before this week is over. I think you'd enjoy it more by auto than by train, anyway. You see more of the scenery that way, I think.

By the way, my landlady said that you could stay with us. You see, they have a room up in the attic (which is very hot in this summer, but would be alrite now) and I could sleep there and you could have my room, so I guess that'll settle that problem.

I'm enclosing 2 dollars. My insurance is due this week, also spent $3.50 for a new battery for my radio. I asked Rum to find out how much they are in Bflo., not that it would make much difference now, but I think I paid a little too much for it.

Well, I guess that's about all for now so will close with

love.

Ed

PS TO RUM: Don't forget to take care of my errands for me. Thanx.

Wednesday – 9:45 PM
October 8, 1941

Dear Mother:

Received your letter yesterday and the laundry last Saturday. I've been quite busy this week. There's a mission at our church this week for men and I'm making it. It lasts from 7:30 until 9 o'clock.

Last nite went to see Gary Cooper in "Sergeant York". I like it very much. It's a true story of Alvin C. York who was drafted for the Army during the first World War, even though he tried to get exemption from Washington, D.C., because war was against his belief. Well, he didn't get exempted and went to France where he became a hero by capturing 132 Germans single-handed. I believe Alvin York was in New York at about the same time that Rum and I were on the 4th of July. You see that's when the picture started in New York City. Incidentally, I went to the show with a girl whose brother was drafted about 2 weeks ago. When they showed the part where Gary Cooper is getting ready to leave home for camp she cried out loud 'cause it reminded her of her brother, and she misses him that much. I've met her whole family and they sure seem very much attached. There are 4 boys and 4 girls, and that's the first time that her brother had been away from home. He's down at Fort Knox, Kentucky.

Last Friday the Warehouse Chief became ill and I was told to take charge of the Warehouse having 7 men under me. I've been told that I'm to be in charge whenever the boss is absent. He gets about $2300 per year. Wish they'd give me a raise along with the responsibility. That seems to be always my trouble. I'm told that my work is very good and then am given responsible tasks but never material appreciation, but then maybe I'm too impatient. Well, time will tell.

Rum is going to move this Friday nite to my former boss's home. I could have had the room but seeing as how we don't know how long we'll be up here and my present room isn't too bad I told Rum to take it. You see the fellow who had the room has been transferred to Staten Island, N. Y. So now Rum and I both will live on a street named after a tree. Rum will live at 25 Maple Street, (even the number is almost the same.)

You didn't give very much information as to Mamie's operation, that is, what the operation was for and who the doctor was. I'm dropping Mamie a card tonite.

I'm enclosing a couple of pictures of "Butch" and I taken just about a month ago. In one of them I had just kissed him and he put his finger in my ear.

About a week from today Massena will be "invaded" by 3,000 soldiers from Pine Camp, who will have war maneuvers here outside of town for 2 weeks. Should be interesting. This town will really be crowded now.

    S'long now with love.

                           Edward

Twenty-Third Street
Young Men's Christian Association
215 West 23rd Street
New York, NY
Telephone Chelsea 3-1982
Member's Correspondence

Monday. 11:20 PM
December 8, 1941

Dear Mother:

Well, since I called you tonite I won't have very much to write but thought I'd drop a few lines anyway.

I'm enclosing picture taken in an office building today. It sure is a madhouse.

I saw the Lucky Strike Hit Parade on Saturday nite and Prudential Family Hour last nite. Wednesday nite we're going to see Glenn Miller at 10 PM on CBS. Friday nite we'll see Cities Service and Lucille Mannus is going to sing "Tales of the Vienna Woods". I've written for some more tickets.

After Henry and I met in Times Square last nite we came back to my room for awhile. He might get a day off next week, so we'll be able to stay out later at nite.

Well, if my leave is approved I'll be leaving N. Y., for Buffalo, two weeks from tomorrow nite.

So long for now.

Love

Ed

P.S. Received your letter this morning. Incidentally I'd still rather have you write to the office instead of here.

Fort McClellan
Anniston
Alabama

Tuesday
9:30 PM
3-3-42

Dear Mother:

Well here I am at one of the U.S.O. places here in Anniston. We got paid today. I received $15.92 and am enclosing $5.00 for you.

Got another shot in the arm today for lockjaw. One more to go and that will be in 3 weeks.

Well, I'd better close as I still have to get back to camp by 11 PM. I'm with 2 other fellows from my tent.

Love

E

Saint Joseph's Church
Varysburg, N.Y.

March 6, 1942

Mrs. J. Bartz
    My Dear Mrs Bartz,

    Thank you very much for your letter of March 4, and the offering of a dollar.

    I shall burn a Vigil Light for the protection of your dear son, Edward.

    Promising to remember him fervently and frequently at the altar, that God may shield him from every danger, with best wishes to you, I remain,

    Very gratefully yours,

    Father Lutz

AMERICAN RED CROSS

Sunday Morn
9:30 o'clock
March 22, '42

Dear Mother:

Yes, I'm really writing this in a hospital bed. Don't worry; I'm alright now, although I guess I was quite a sick boy on Tues., Wed., & Thurs., though not serious enough for them to notify you.

Seems strange how my hunches still come true. Last Sunday I didn't feel too well and mentioned to Mamie and Lillian that I might be getting the "flu". On Monday I was told told to stay in my tent all day and in bed. On Tuesday, the doctor said I had influenza and the ambulance took me over to the hospital here. For 3 days I thought I was floating around thru space. They give Sulfanilamide tablets every 4 hours (even awaken me at nite). To prevent pneumonia I guess.

There are 33 other fellows in this ward and believe it or not, most of them from New York City! So I have a lot to talk about to them. Seems there's all city fellows here. Couldn't take it I guess.

My basic training was supposed to be finished on Easter Sunday, but now I don't know. Of course, I've taken the most important part of my training. There are also other fellows from my Company, in the hospital. Almost 10 of them. One of them landed in the hospital 4 days after we arrived here.

The "Angels of Mercy" are pretty good around here. They try to keep us cheered up.

Seems strange…I remember way back in 1917 when I wore a mask to avoid getting the "flu" and here 25 years later, I am more than a 1000 miles from home in an Army hospital with the "flu".

All I need is 2 weeks either in Kane, Pa., or Saranac Lake, N. Y., and I'd be O.K. This air here is very damp.

That was another hunch I had: That I'd be sent here.

But I can't seem to get a hunch as to where I'll go after I leave here. I don't know just how long I'll have to stay here. Rite now I feel as strong as a 3-day kitten.

In regards to mail. I guess you'd better address same as before. Then they will send it to me all at once, I guess.

I won't write any more letters today.

You can tell Lillian I'll write to her after I get a letter from her first. The last one from her was "the" letter. She'll know what you mean. Maybe the mail is being held up at my Company. You know how the Army works. So long for now and let me hear from you.

Love,

Ed

P.S. Please ask Mamie to send stamps. I had to borrow this one.

(Envelope post-marked)

March 28, 1942, 8 AM
Varysburg, N.Y.

(Printed Card)

My Mass at dawn on Easter Sunday morning will be offered for the spiritual and temporal welfare of my friends among whom you are affectionately remembered.

Father Lutz

Saint Joseph's Church
Varysburg, N.Y.

(Envelope post-marked)
April 5, 1943, 3 PM
Varysburg, N.Y.

St. Joseph's Church
Varysburg, N.Y.

Dear Friend – Mrs. Bartz,

Thank you very much for your favor. Assuring you that your generosity has been deeply appreciated, with sincerest best wishes to you and yours, hoping to see you soon, I remain, Fervently shall I continue to remember Edward at the altar, that God, some day, will bring him back in good health and happy. May you enjoy a Happy Easter.

Father Lutz

United States Army
Fort Benning, Georgia

Monday Evening
7:30 o'clock
Apr. 27, 1942

Dear Mother:

The mail is still working very strangely here at Benning. This morning received your Thursday and Friday nite letters, which were very good service. This afternoon received your Tuesday letter with the $1.00 in it. The wrist watch has not as yet come, although you sent it out a week ago. Did you have it insured?

Last week I send Father Lutz a short note telling him that I was transferred here and liked it very much. Received a short note from him today which read: "Am glad you are happy and contented. That God may ever be with you, is my sincerest prayer". He also enclosed a religious card and a very nice one. The American flag is in the background; in front of it is Jesus and in front of Him are a soldier and a sailor.

If you haven't as yet sent out my khaki shirt, I'd also like you to send me all my white sox. They should be much cooler. I'm going to wear my civilian shoes from now on as the high Army shoes are too warm. We're allowed to wear civilian shoes as long as they're military looking. At McClellan we weren't allowed to wear them.

Thanks for sending me the vitamin capsules. Wonder how many weeks it'll take for them to arrive? Yes, I'm feeling much better every day and am gaining weight. Don't know how much I weigh right now, but I'll let you know as soon as I find out.

Yes, when I type in the evening or Sundays I do it right here in the Barracks in the 1st Sergeant's room. He lets me use it, but I think I'm going to start writing my letters on the roof, so I can be outdoors and still get my letters written.

Never mind sending me anymore money. We get paid on April 30th and also Rum sent me $10.00 yesterday.

You said you inquired about train fare, etc., and said you'd change at Cincinatti, O., Washington, Atlanta, Ga. I can't figure out why you should go thru Washington, D.C. I still think you'd get tired out on the bus, but it's up to you. You know it'll be about 1100 miles and the bus takes much longer apparently, if you say 41 hours. The train I guess takes about 19. I could meet you at Columbus and take the bus from there to here.

Well, that's all for now.

Love,
Ed

St. Joseph's Church
Varysburg, N.Y.

Postcard Post-marked
May 14, 1942
5 PM

Dear Friend – Mrs. Bartz,

Thank you very much for your favor. Assuring you that your generosity has been deeply appreciated, with sincerest best wishes to you and yours, hoping to see you soon, I remain, am very glad it is going well with Edward. Will be glad also to do as you request in your letter of May 11.

Father Lutz

Fort Benning
Georgia

Monday Nite
8:00 o'clock
May 18, 1942

Dear Mother:

Received your Thursday letter today. Thanks for the $1.00 bill.

It's too bad you could not have got more allowance on my wrist watch, but with the name on it, I guess you couldn't very well. I'll sure be glad to get it. As you know the Army is run on schedule and I have to ask someone what time it is at least 10 times a day.

I'm really beginning to feel healthy now. Full of pep all the while. When the bugle sounds at 5:45 AM I'm usually the first one up in the room.

I guess Mamie isn't too well satisfied with her job. But I told her to be patient. Remember I didn't like it at first either but later did very much. How do you like this stationery? It's a better grade than the others I had. When you address me, you don't have to put the ISSC on the envelope.

I must be getting younger looking or something. One of the girls in the office thought I was about 19 or 20 years old. The fellows down South seem to look older than their age. Maybe 'cause they don't exercise very much,

So long for now.

Love and kissed

Ed

Sergeant Edward F. Bartz
Academic Regiment, Company A
Fort Benning, Georgia

Sunday
June 7, '42

Dear Mother:

It just dawned on me how fast time is flying. Here's what I mean: in case my furlough is approved I'll be leaving either a week from tomorrow nite or Tuesday morning and I don't have enough money to buy the train fare. Will you please send me about $25.00 (money order) as soon as you get this letter, if possible. You need not send it via Special Delivery but you'd better send via Air Mail. I can't wait until the furlough is approved 'cause that might be at the last minute, as such things happen in the Army. Want to buy RR ticked ahead.

I guess I'll go over to the Railroad station in Columbus tonite and see how much more the fare would be to go by way of New York City. If there's too much difference in time and money I'll abandon the idea I guess.

Received your Wednesday nite letter, addressing me as Sgt., yesterday. Also the laundry bags, shirt and 'kerchiefs. Thanks a lot. I'm glad that you put the ropes in the tops of the bags. I forgot to ask you to do that but you did it anyway. I can use the small bag some week when I don't happen to have very much laundry. (Which won't be in the summertime).

The fellows here are all surprised that I got promoted to Sergeant so quickly. Usually they become Private First Class or maybe even a Corporal. Some have been here a year and a half and are Corporals. I guess I was just lucky and got the breaks. I remember on the morning of February 2nd as I was leaving for the Induction Station and shook hands with Freeman; he said "look for breaks". So I guess I just followed his advice.

So long for now and hope I'll be able to see you in about 10 or 11 days.

Love and Kisses

Ed

P.S. Just got a letter from Rum. He's waiting to take a leave if I get a furlough.

Two More Promotions

FT. BENNING, Ga.—Two Buffalo men have been promoted. Earl B. Miller, son of Mr. and Mrs. Herman Nickles of 111 Woodlawn ave., was promoted to sergeant from corporal. Edward F. Bartz, son of Mrs. Josephine Bartz of 497 Riley st., was promoted from private to sergeant. He is with A Company of the Academic Regiment.

Sgt. Edward F. Bartz
Academic Regt, Company A
Fort Benning, Georgia

Monday
June 8, '42
7:55 PM

Dear Mother:

Received your Thursday nite letter and also card of congratulations. Thanks.

Nothing new about my furlough as yet. Went over to the R.R., station in Columbus last nite. The train leaves here at 3:50 pm and I'd be home at 8:59 PM the next day. Still don't know about going to New York. Trip there is about 22 hours, then 8 hours from there to Bflo. Furlough fare from Columbus to Buffalo, via Cincinnatti, is $25.60.

That's all for now. G'nite.

Love,

Ed

Private Edward F. Bartz
Academic Bn., Company A
Fort Benning, Georgia

Friday Evening
7:25 o'clock
June 12, 1942

Dear Mother:

Received your Wednesday nite letter with $5.00 today and yesterday got the $30.00 money order which Freeman sent. Thanks. I still don't have any information as to my furlough. I guess they're wondering who'd take my place while I was away. Three other fellows who came down with me from Ft. McClellan and who work in the same building got promotions, but they were made Corporals. Also they have applied for furloughs and have all been approved. They are either typists or file clerks. I don't type anymore or do any filing, but mostly supervise work of others. Well, I'm still hoping that I get the furlough.

Also received letters from Rum, Mamie and Al today. Rum was supposed to go to Buffalo this weekend, but when he received my letter he postponed it till next weekend (June 19-22).

Well, it looks as if the new Pay Bill will finally go thru. I've decided to have them deduct $18.75 each month from my pay and buy a bond. That still will leave me almost $60.00 with the new pay. As soon as I fill out the application for purchasing the bonds I'll tell them to send them home to you, for keeping.

Yes, I noticed the item about my promotion in Saturday's Buflo News. Will get Wednesday's news tomorrow probably so I'll see the 2nd item. I'm enclosing negatives of the picnic (which the girl at the office finally returned). I guess you have the pictures.

Mamie told me in her letter that she left my picture, in uniform, at the News and that it'd be about 2 or 3 weeks more before it appeared in print.

Well, that's all for now and hope I'll see you shortly after you get this letter.

Love and Kisses,
Ed

Saturday, June 6, 1942

With the Buffalo Boys in Camp

Wagner Now Lieutenant

Special to the Buffalo Evening News.

CAMP DAVIS, N. C.—Theodore J. Wagner, 88 Box ave., Buffalo, was commissioned a second lieutenant after completing officer-candidate school here.

Buffalo Man Is Technician

FT. KNOX, Ky.—Jerome L. Lenhard, 36 Colfax ave., Buffalo, attending the mechanical school here, is now a technician, third grade.

Soldier Is Transferred

INILCENE, Wash.—Private First Class Art Hann, 256 Baynes st., Buffalo, has been transferred to Ft. Benning, Ga., for the motor mechanics training course.

To Complete Flight Training

AUGUSTA, Ga.—John F. Wukas Jr., 95 Custer st., Buffalo, has completed his course at Gunter Field here and will soon be assigned to another field for final flight training.

Three Obtain Commissions

FT. BELVOIR, Va.—The following Buffalonians completed the engineer officer-candidate school course and were commissioned second lieutenants: Richard H. Baer, Martin J. Pleuthner, Eugene H. Plumacher.

Lieut. DeLisle Appointed

PINE CAMP—Lieut. Ramson H. DeLisle, who served ten years in the New York Central divisional engineer's office in Buffalo, has been appointed new post engineering property and contracting officer here.

Assigned to Medical Units

CAMP GRANT, Ill.—First Lieut. Russell E. Reitz, 1048 East Ferry st., and Lieut. Joseph T. Andrews, 563 Riley st., Buffalo, have been assigned to the medical training battalions here.

Soldier at Cavalry School

FT. RILEY, Kan.—Private George H. Mattison, 654 Woodlawn ave., Buffalo, has reported at the cavalry school here.

Sergeant at Infantry School

FT. BENNING, Ga.—Assigned to the office of the Infantry School here, Private Edward F. Bartz recently was promoted to sergeant. He is the son of Mrs. Josephine Bartz, 497 Riley st.

Cadet Flanagan Commissioned

WAYNE, Pa.—John G. Flanagan, son of Mr. and Mrs. John J. Flanagan of 90 Dana rd., Buffalo, was among 27 cadets of the Valley Forge Military Academy here to be commissioned recently as second lieutenants in the Army Reserve Corps, subject to active duty beginning June 10.

Buffalo Girl to Graduate

Special to the Buffalo Evening News.

BRADFORD, Mass., June 6.—Miss Elizabeth Gerner, daughter of Mr. and Mrs. Philip H. Gerner, 322 Woodbridge ave., Buffalo, will be graduated Monday from Bradford Junior College here.

Wednesday Evening
21:21 o'clock
July 1st, 1942

Dear Mother:

Received your Saturday nite letter yesterday. Did you notice the time I have above? Effective today the Army is going to use the 24 hour system. That is we start with 1 in the morning and continue on. 1 in the afternoon is 13 o'clock and so on. 12 midnite is 24 o'clock. So now it's just about 25 minutes after 21 o'clock or to you civilians it's 9:25 PM. Now we don't have to us AM or PM at all. I suppose you noticed that my train to New York left at 11 o'clock supposed to depart until 11:10. Do you know why? That is the 9:30 train and was 1-1/2 hours late. We arrived in N.Y., at 7 PM. Immediately checked in at the Commodore Hotel and got a 20% discount 'cause of being in the service. It sure was nice to see N. Y., again and I was really glad I went. Had my uniform pressed, shaved and took a shower. Then went to pick up the girl on Park ave. She wore a formal gown and we went up to the Astor Roof dancing to the orchestra of Tommy Dorsey. It was very good. Got back at 4:30 AM. Had the operator call me at 8:30 AM. Then on the subway at 270 Broadway to see the people I know at the Engineering office. Sure was nice to see them. Also called Bob Pawlowski up. Incidentally, I hardly recognized Times Square on Friday nite, as most of the lights are out and it's quite dark.

I left New York City at 6:30 PM Saturday, arriving in Washington, D.C., at 10:25 after having gone thru New York, New Jersey, Pennsylvania, Delaware, Maryland and District of Columbia in less than 4 hours. The next train did not leave until one hour later. So I grabbed a bite to eat at Union Station; then at 11 o'clock I tried to call you. It would only have cost 70(cents). But I guess you must have gone to Adeline's as I notice your letter was written at 9:20 PM and you said that Butch was with you, so you apparently took him home.

I didn't sleep very much going down. We went thru the states of Virginia, North Carolina and South Carolina. Virginia is a very pretty state. I was just thinking, up to July 1940 I had only been in the states of New York and Pennsylvania. Since then I've been in:

Ohio	New Jersey	Georgia	Tennessee
Michigan	Maryland	Alabama	D. of C.
Indiana	Delaware	North Carolina	
Kentucky	Virginia	South Carolina	

We arrived in Columbus at 9:15 Sunday nite. Arrived in camp at 10:10 as had to wait for a bus. Went to sleep before touching the pillow. Have been in bed Monday and last nite at 9:30 and am catching up on my sleep. There were 10 letters for me and about 12 papers. Incidentally, received a letter from one my old girl friends, who's married and has a child by now. It seems she saw my picture in the News and so addressed me just at Ft. Benning, but I got it alright after some delay. Wants me to write back.

Things were sure changed around here. It seems they always did change when I went home from Massena. But this time things went for the better. My job has been taken over by a Corporal, BUT I've taken a Staff Sergeant's job. It's much more complicated and responsible but I guess I'll manage alright. I may even get another promotion to Staff Sgt., in a short while, but am not too sure as yet. That would give me about $94 per month. Seems strange that they should give me a better job after I had been gone for 11 days.

Incidentally, we won't get paid until July 10th as a new pay roll is being made up because of the pay increase. I don't know whether Lillian will be around to see you or not; I wrote to her tonite saying that I thought it best that we be just "friends". Guess it'd be better if you don't show her this letter. I never cared very much for that idea, anyway, of you showing her my letters.

Well, I'd better close now as it's almost 22 o'clock and I want to get some sleep.

Love & Kisses

Edward

Sgt. Edw. F. Bartz
Company "A"
Academic Regiment
Ft. Benning, Georgia

Saturday
042340Z
1942

Dear Mother:

The numbers above under Saturday tell me that it's July 4th and the time is 7:40 PM. The last time I wrote you I made a little mistake in interpreting the time. You see, we go right around the clock to 24, but always add 4 hours to it, which makes it Greenwich Civil Time. So that when it's 8 PM here it's actually 20 o'clock Eastern War Time in the Army, but we use GCT which makes it 24 PM. Does it sound complicated? It did to me too at first, but it's very simple now.

Well, I have been told that I have been recommended for promotion to Staff Sergeant. I could hardly believe it, as I only got my promotion to Sergeant a month ago. The fellows don't think that it will be approved as I haven't been in the Army long enough. They've never heard of a fellow becoming a Staff Sergeant in only 5 months in the Army. They were pretty much surprised when I became Sergeant in 4 months. I'm wondering whether it'll be approved, but rather think that I won't as that's pretty quick promotion. If I should get it my pay would be $96 per month. Also once a soldier becomes a Staff Sergeant or higher, if he should get married he gets extra allowance for rations, etc. Which means that if I was a Staff Sergeant and got married, I would get $146.50 per month, which is better than I was earning in civilian life.

We sure have been busy lately. Last nite 4 of us fellows had to go back and work from 6:30 to 9 o'clock. Tomorrow, Sunday, we will work from 9 AM until noon. As today is the 4th of July we only worked from 8 AM to 5 PM.

Received the Massena Observer and there sure was a lot of news of interest to me. First of all, there's one man who worked for the Engineers when I did and he and I ate at the same place. I remember he told me in March 1941 that his son went into the Air Corps. Well, he was killed in a crash last week. The other item concerns Irene Lamour who used to write to me until about 2 months ago. She's getting married this month to some Lieutenant from Georgia, whom she met in California. Also enclosing item about Captain, I mean Major Sibley. When I was in New York they told me that he had malaria, but there was no truth to the item about his boat being sunk. BUT, one of the other fellows, who also contracted malaria, was returning to the

U.S., and the boat was torpedoed and he was badly hurt and is now somewhere in South America. I know the fellow very well, as he worked in Massena.

Received the shoes earlier this week and the clothes today. Also 2 letters from you. Thanks. I suppose as I write this you're going to the show at Civic Stadium, it's 7:55 now.

Instead of having chicken on Sundays and Wednesdays, we now have duck and I like it much better. Today each soldier received a pack of Camels at lunchtime, with a card saying "4th of July greetings from the Mess". This evening at supper each one of us got almost ¼ of watermelon.

Well, I'll close now and if I don't write too often it's because I'm very busy and it's pretty hot. So long.

Love and kisses

Ed

Article:

Major Sibley Still in Africa

Major Alden K. Sibley and his assistant,
Major Allen Henderson, are still in Africa,
according to word received by friends here.
The rumor that the two men were on
a boat which was torpedoed was false. The men
are working out of Cairo, Egypt. Major Sibley has
been ill.

BUFFALO EVENING NEWS—Wednesday, August 12, 1942

TAKE CARE OF YOURSELF, SOLDIER!

Here's How—as Taught in Combat Course at Infantry Officers' School in Georgia

A tricky snare among the many illustrated in the Ft. Benning infantry officers' school combat course, is the "innocent" cabin in a field. A student soldier approaches, is fired upon from inside it (left, above) by a man who runs out, hides in field behind house. Student runs after him is promptly shot in the back (right, above) by second man, concealed in cabin.

After taking Ft. Benning combat course, the soldier knows better. Situation: the same as before—he's fired upon by man who runs into field. Now, soldier first demolishes house with hand grenades (left, above), just in case his foe has a hidden pal, follows up with bayonet charge (right, above), to make sure his job is complete. Only then does he try to track down man who fired at him.

Most difficult maneuver is the log bridge over a stream. Student is concentrating on balance where "enemy" rises from underbrush (left, above), shoots at him. Some men try to finish crossing before attempting to engage enemy. In real combat, this would be fatal. Best idea is to fire from hip (right, above), then continue crossing.

Real "sucker" bait is the log fence. Soldier-students climb fence, and are fired at, just as they reach the top, by "enemy" riflemen hidden on far side. Some students leave rifle on near side while they climb (left, above), but find themselves helpless targets. Others get "smart," place rifle on far side before climbing up. Enemy shots catch them before they reach the top. Best technique is to take rifle along, be in position to blast back at foe (right, above), wipe him out before he can fire a second shot.

Envelope post-marked
Cooperstown, NY
July 27, 1942
5 PM

Am sending money orders tomorrow because I can't get to the post office right now and I need the sheets or the word to buy some.

Rum

Cooperstown, N.Y.
July 23, 1942

Dear Mother:

Just a short letter as I just wrote the other day.

Today I'm moving out my room and going to live in a whole house with 2 other fellows. The place we have consists of five bedrooms and about a half of dozen other rooms. One of the fellows is a good cook and he's going to prepare 2 meals a day. The whole works is furnished except for bed linen and towels. I was wondering if you had any old bed sheets, instead of my buying them. I'd need about 4 or 3 sheets and about 4 pillow cases. Also some towels and wash cloths. That'll be all I need. If you just have good ones I could purchase some cheap ones. The whole place costs $50.00 dollars a month, including electricity. That'll be less than I was paying in Massena. The meals will hardly cost anything and with my $3.00 a day I'll be sitting pretty.

Tell me when you are coming. I suggest you come about the 2nd week in August and stay for about a week. I'll get the train schedule, etc., and send it to you as soon as you make up your mind. Bring Butch along because there is plenty of room.

I received 2 letters from Ed today. One was about 10 days old. It went to Massena, Canton, Ogdensburg and finally reached Cooperstown.

I quit my checking account in Massena and am sending my surplus money to you. Take what you need and when I get home I'll deposit it in the bank. My account book is home but I don't think you can put it in without my signature. If you can make some arrangements, do so. Don't put it in defense bonds because I might need some ready cash. There are 2 money orders, one for a hundred dollars and another one for 80 dollars. I guess I wrote a longer letter then I expected.

Send my stuff to U. S. Engineer Office, because no one will ever be at the house during the day.

Love,

Rum

Staff Sergeant Edward F. Bartz
Academic Regt., Company A
Fort Benning, Georgia

Friday Evening
9:45 o'clock
Aug. 14, 1942

Dear Mother:

Have received your letters and also the Congratulations card with $5.00. Thanks!

Received Tuesday's News today and saw my name in the promotions list. Wonder if they'll send me cigarettes or cigars, since you send in my name for "smokes".

I am now a Squad Leader and have to report my men in each morning. Also have to see that cleanup work is done right. Have charge of about 14 men.

Still buying peaches and they're the best I've ever eaten. Must be because they're out in the sun longer, than those shipped up North. I now make $96.00 per month or $3.20 per day. At Massena I made $4.00 per day, but had a lot of expenses.

I suppose you'll get this letter just before leaving for Cooperstown. Are you taking Butch with you?

So long for now and have a good time.

Love & Kisses

Ed

10:10 A.M.
Sept. 2, 1942

Dear Mother:

Just got lunch from town. Went down with Eleanor while Mamie was still sleeping. I like to get out and walk real early in the morning. Usually get up at 6 or 7, so does Eleanor.

This place is swell. I'd like to live here as the people are so different from the ones in Buffalo.

Mamie and Eleanor went boat-riding yesterday while I sat on the beach and watched them. The man with the goatee sat down on the same beach and told me all about Cooperstown and told about the places we should go to see while we're here. He's lived here 75 years.

We listened to the program from Fort Benning, but didn't think it was so good.

We're having perfect weather here. The mornings and nites are cold, but during the (day) it's hot.

I made Rum's breakfast and lunch and we eat out in the evening. The corn is delicious. I ate 5 ears yesterday and bought some more this morning for our lunch.

We've changed our mind about coming home Sunday and are coming home Saturday nite instead as Joe, the Italian fellow is getting company over the Labor Day weekend and Rum said that it's better that we leave Saturday as Joe and his company will want to have the place to themselves. So we'll be in Buffalo at 11:15 P.M. at the N.Y.C. Station on Sat. nite. If you want to you can bring the kids home Sat. nite and let them sleep home. Better get something for Sunday dinner as I won't be able to get anything.

Love,

Adeline (O'Hara)

The Robert Fulton Hotel
Atlanta, GA.

Saturday
4:20 pm
Sept. 26, '42

Dear Mother:

Here on the bus, after leaving Columbus at 12 noon. This is where I stayed while enroute home in June.

The fellow who came with me from Ft. McClellan also is with me.

Don't know what we'll do yet. It's raining right now and quite cool.

Love 'n Kisses

Ed

Addresses of Those in Service Are Requested by News Smokes-Fund

Have you sent names and addresses of members of your immediate family serving with the armed force of the United States to the Buffalo Evening News Smokes-for-Soldiers Fund?

To facilitate the further distribution of cigars and cigarettes to Buffalo and Western New York men in the Army, Navy, Marine Corps and Coast Guard the Buffalo Evening News invites residents of the eight counties of Western New York to submit this information.

It is requested that only names and addresses of members of a household be sent in order to avoid duplication. (Do not send names of nephews, cousins, grandchildren or friends unless they actually live in your home.)

When submitting names of men eligible to receive smokes from the Buffalo Evening News Smokes-Fund, please print carefully the following information:

1. Rank and full name.
2. Identification number, if known.
3. Postoffice mailing address.
4. Legal residence (address of man at time of enlistment or induction.)
5. Name and address of person submitting information.

This information may be submitted on a postal card or in a letter. Be sure that information may be clearly read. Address this information to Buffalo Evening News Smokes-for-Soldiers Fund, Buffalo, N. Y. Telephone calls cannot be accepted.

WEDNESDAY EVENING
DECEMBER 2, 1942
7:30 o'clock

DEAR MOTHER:
HAVE YOUR TWO LETTERS WHICH ARRIVED THIS
WEEK. I'VE BEEN OUT FOR THE PAST TWO NIGHTS SO
THOUGHT I'D STAY IN TONITE AND CATCH UP ON SOME OF
MY CORRESPONDENCE.
WE WERE PAID ON MONDAY. MY PAY AMOUNTED TO
$122.85. OF COURSE, $18.75 WAS DEDUCTED FOR THE BOND,
$1.50 FOR LAUNDRY AND $1.38 FOR INSURANCE, LEAVING
ME $101.22 IN CASH. I'VE BEEN CARRYING IT AROUND FOR
3 DAYS SO THOUGHT I'D START SENDING SOME OF IT
TONIGHT AND GOT SOME MONEY ORDERS. I'M ENCLOSING
$25.00 FOR YOU; ALSO SENDING $15.00 TO MAMIE TO GIVE
TO WALLY FOR CHANGING OF THE NAME; ALSO SENDING
$10.00 TO RUM WHICH I HAD BORROWED FROM HIM. SO
THAT LEAVES ME A LITTLE OVER $50.00. I THOUGHT I'D
KEEP THAT MUCH FOR CHRISTMAS SHOPPING, ALTHOUGH
I DON'T KNOW WHEN I'LL BE ABLE TO DO IT. NO, I'M
NOT GIVING ANY PRESENTS TO ANY GIRLS THIS YEAR
AS I'M NOT SERIOUS ABOUT ANYONE IN PARTICULAR.
INCIDENTALLY, I'M GOING OUT WITH ANOTHER GIRL, BY
NAME OF JOSEPHINE WRIGHT. HER HOME IS IN A LITTLE
TOWN ABOUT 40 MILES FROM HERE, BUT SHE ROOMS WITH
HER AUNT AND UNCLE IN COLUMBUS. VERY NICE GIRL AND
GOOD COMPANY. YES, I ALSO STILL GO WITH DORIS.
YOU MENTIONED HAVING LOTS OF SNOW IN
BUFFALO. I DON'T THINK WE'LL HAVE ANY AT ALL, AS
SNOW IS QUITE RARE IN THIS PART OF GEORGIA.
IN REGARD TO THE "LIFE" MAGAZINE WHICH YOU
MENTIONED IN YOUR LAST LETTER, FOR GIVING ME AT
XMAS TIME. MAMIE HAD PREVIOUSLY ASKED ME FOR
SOME GIFT SUGGESTIONS
AND I HAD MENTIONED, AMONG OTHER THINGS, A
SUBSCRIPTION TO "TIME" MAGAZINE, ALSO WEEKLY. IT
REALLY IS VERY GOOD READING AND CONTAINS THE
NEWS OF THE WEEK VERY WELL WRITTEN. IT'S 15(CENTS)
PER COPY AND THE YEARLY SUBSCRIPTION IS $5.00. I
DON'T KNOW WHETHER THERE'S A REDUCED RATE FOR
SOLDIERS OR NOT. I ALREADY HAVE A SUBSCRIPTION TO
THE "READERS DIGEST" WHICH LILLIAN GOT FOR ME
LAST JUNE. I GET A CHANCE TO SEE "LIFE" MAGAZINE
HERE AT COMPANY DAYROOM EACH WEEK. I WAS RATHER

SHOCKED TO READ TODAY IN THE MASSENA PAPER THAT
WILFRED MYERS WAS KILLED IN AN AUTO ACCIDENT
LAST WEEK. HE'S THE ONE AT WHOSE HOME I LIVED AT
27 WALNUT AVENUE, MASSENA., AND ONE OF THE LAST
PERSONS I SAW BEFORE I LEFT MASSENA FOR BUFFALO
AND THE ARMY LAST JANUARY. IT SEEMS THAT HIS CAR
HAD GONE OFF THE ROAD AND HIT A TREE SOMETIME
DURING THE NIGHT, BUT HE WASN'T DISCOVERED UNTIL
THE NEXT MORNING, BUT HAD APPARENTLY BEEN KILLED
INSTANTLY. I THINK HIS WIFE WAS WORKING IN BUFFALO.
THEY DIDN'T SEEM TO GET ALONG TOGETHER VERY
WELL. HE WAS 40 AND SHE'S ABOUT 23. I'M QUITE SURE
THAT I WON'T BE ABLE TO BE HOME FOR CHRISTMAS, AS
THEY'RE NOT GIVING FURLOUGHS TO ANYONE IN THE
ADJUTANT GENERAL'S OFFICE. EVEN THE CIVILIANS CAN'T
GET MORE THAN 2 DAYS OFF. I'M GOING TO TRY AND GET
ONE SOMETIME IN JANUARY. INCIDENTALLY, TODAY MARKS
10 MONTHS SINCE MY INDUCTION INTO THE ARMY. IT
SURE HAS GONE FAST
     WELL, THAT'S ABOUT ALL FOR NOW. INCIDENTALLY,
I'VE GOT AN INVITATION TO DINNER FOR TOMORROW
NIGHT. HERE AT THE BARRACKS TONITE WE HAD LIVER
AND BELIEVE ME THAT'S THE BEST LIVER I EVER ATE. I
REALLY LIKED IT.

Love and kisses

Ed

PS: INCIDENTALLY, TODAY HERE AT THE COMPANY
WE WERE GIVEN FORMS TO FILL OUT IN REGARDS TO
WHERE PARENTS WERE BORN, ALSO WHETHER WE HAVE
ANY RELATIVES LIVING IN FOREIGN COUNTRIES. I GUESS
THE INTELLIGENCE OFFICER IS DOING SOME CHECKING
UP. WE HAVE SEVERAL FELLOWS HERE WHO ARE NOT U. S.
CITIZENS. SEEMS STRANGE THEY CAN BE IN THE ARMY AS
ENLISTED MEN BUT NOT AS OFFICERS.

The Bankhead Hotel
Birmingham, Alabama

Sunday
December 6, 1942

Dear Mother:

Came down here with two other sergeants yesterday. Birmingham is about 170 miles from Ft. Benning and it took us about 5 hours to come down here by train. One of the fellows is from Hawaii and attended school at Benning but did not graduate so now he's in Company "A". Anyway, he has some friends here in Birmingham, a couple of doctors and their wives, who also formerly lived in Hawaii. So we were at a party last nite and had a good time. My head is several sizes too large this morning. Went to church this morning and after Mass they give free breakfast to soldiers in the school hall, served by very pretty girls. This is a very hospitable city. We also got invitations to go to a dinner today, but we have other plans to see the people with whom we were last nite, so we couldn't accept. I'm going to come here more often I think, but I'll have to take more time off, as we didn't arrive here last nite until 9:30 o'clock; and left Columbus at 4:30.

So long for now.

Love

Ed

Mon eve – 10:45 P.M.
December 14, 1942
Cooperstown, New York

Dear Mother:

Just returned from bowling. It was league night tonight but our team didn't do so good. We are still near the top of the league however.

It's gotten quite cold here lately. This morning the temperature was exactly zero and there's plenty of snow which fell Saturday night and all day Sunday.

I sent Sonny and his wife a congratulations card.

I'll probably be home for Christmas. However the problem will be how to get there. The trains will be plenty crowded and I might not be able to buy a ticket. I think tho that I'll make it somehow and it'll be Christmas Eve at about 11:00 or 12:00 o'clock at night. There is a possibility that I might make it a day before but I doubt it.

Do you know what I could get for Mamie? Or could you get it? Does she use perfume or need any? I would get that here.

Just a little more than a month's time and we'll be out of Cooperstown. I had previously planned to go to Panama, Cuba and South America but I never got there. Now I'm thinking of going to Canada to work on the Alaskan Highway. The place in Canada is called Edmonton and is about 600 miles north of the border and about 500 from the Pacific Coast. If I go there I'll get a substantial raise. It's very cold up there however.

I received the laundry this past Thursday.

Well that's about all for now. I received a check from New York today made out to Ed. It's his overtime for last New Years day I believe and I'll send that off tonight too while I'm in the writing mood more or less.

Enclosed is $25.00 to buy Christmas presents and stuff.

Love

Rum

Left to right:
Sgt. Robb
S/Sgt. Frazier
me
Sgt. Daniel
12-20-4?

Saint Joseph's Church
Varysburg, N.Y.
Dec. 18, 1942

Mrs. J. Bartz
My Dear Mrs. Bartz,

    Today I received a Christmas card from your son, Edward, and he has been promoted to St. Sgt. Heartiest congratulations!

    Assuring you, that he shall be frequently and fervently remembered at the altar, that when this struggle is ended, he may return to us enjoying health and happiness, wishing you a Merry Christmas and a Happy New Year, I remain,

           Very sincerely yours,

    Father Lutz

St. Joseph's Church
Varysburg, N.Y.
Postmarked Jan 2, 1943

Dear Friend: - Mrs. Bartz,

Thank you very much for your favor. Assuring you that your generosity has been deeply appreciated, with sincerest best wishes to you and yours, hoping to see you soon, I remain, am referring to your donation and New Year Greeting you mailed, Dec. 29. May the New Year be a happy one for you and yours. May God especially protect your son, Edward.

Father Lutz

Ward A-1
Station Hospital
Wednesday
January 6, 1943

Dear Mother:

Yes, here I am again in a hospital! Only this time I've got pneumonia. You need not worry though as I'm out of danger now. I've been here since 9 AM on December 31st.

I caught a cold about 10 days before Christmas. The afternoon of Dec. 30th I left the office at 5 instead of 5:30, as I felt rather low. The next morning I ached all over and had a high temperature, so reported to the Dispensary for sick call. There the doctor took my temperature and examined me and then said "you're going to the hospital, Sergeant." So they took me in an ambulance. At the hospital I was put in a ward with about 25 other soldiers. Next day, which was New Year's Day, I got worse and they moved me into a private room. Then they got the portable X-Ray machine and took a shot of my chest. Later the report came back saying I had "pneumonia in left lung."

I didn't eat a thing for 2 days, only had liquids. I guess at one time my temperature was near 104 (degrees) and I was seeing animals all over the walls and ceiling.

I still am not allowed to get out of bed. One of the nurses brought me this stationery and I'm propped up in bed.

You should have seen the beard I had until yesterday.

My friends have been coming in to see me, but of course, can't stay long. Monday night one of the fellows brought 5-lb box of candy which you sent. I had it passed around and sent it back, for him to pass around the barracks. I can't eat it.

Last night one of the fellows brought my wrist watch over. Also have your letter which you wrote New Year's Eve.

Well, I should be home pretty soon, as I understand that soldiers get at least 15-day convalescent furloughs after either pneumonia or appendicitis.

I feel pretty good, except that I'm still quite weak.

The only reason I can find for having got this is overwork, as I hadn't gone out very much. At the office I had to work hard, nights & Sundays. Finally, they got me more help but it was too late. Before they wouldn't have given me a 3-day pass; now I'll be gone for awhile I guess.

Well, so long, Mother, and don't worry about anything and I'll see you soon.

my address:
Ward A-1
Station Hospital

Love & Kisses

Ed

Happy Birthday to Adeline!

1:50 pm

P.S. Received your package with fountain pen, etc., on Dec. 29. Wrote letter but not mailed yet.

Wednesday – January 13, 1943
11:00 P. M.
Cooperstown, New York

Dear Mother:

I imagine it's about time that I wrote and told you that I arrived safe and sound in Cooperstown about 17 days ago.

The train pulled into Syracuse about 7:00, over an hour and a half late. I dozed off in the train but didn't rest too well. The coaches were very crowded too, hot and stuffy. There wasn't a vacant seat either. I almost suffocated with my cold. Arrived in Cooperstown about 11:00 Monday Morning due to bad roads, fallen trees and wires caused by a terrific storm the night before.

Back in Cooperstown I got rid of my cold in about 2 days. This climate must be the kind of air I need.

I bought a pair of skis and skiing outfit about 2 weeks ago. Been skiing 3 times now and it's a lot of fun. There are some swell slopes around this part of the country.

Had a letter from Ed the other day, telling me he's recuperating again in the hospital.

Received the laundry last Thursday with everything in fine shape.

Might know where I'll be going soon. At any rate I'll be home if Ed gets the funds he expects or when I leave Cooperstown which is less than 3 weeks time now. Maybe you had better send the traveling bag as I might need it soon. I'll send my other excess baggage by express one of these days.

Love,

Rum

Staff Sgt. Edward F. Bartz
Ward A-1
Station Hospital
Fort Benning, Georgia

January 13, '43

Dear Mother:

After I had been here in the hospital for several days, the fellows told me that a package had arrived for me at the barracks, about the same day I took ill. I told them to hold it for me till I returned, as they said it was quite large.

A couple days ago I got to thinking that it might be perishable, although they said it wasn't marked that way. So last night one of the fellows brought it up. It was from Harriet; Containing oranges, apples, grapes, candy, nuts, fruit cake, chewing gum. Yes, the fruit sure was spoiled, except for one apple. She sure sent me a lot of things. A 1-lb. box of good chocolates, 1-lb. salted nuts in a vacuum packed jar, several packs of gum, etc. She seems to remember me, even if she is married.

Incidentally, Lillian wrote and said she's engaged to that fellow "Jug". Doesn't bother me at all.

Am feeling better each day, but still in bed. The News sent out a flat-fifty of Camels but of course I can't smoke. Gave them to a friend.

So long for now.

Love & Kisses

Ed

Tuesday – 2:45 P.M.
January 19, 1943
Cooperstown

Dear Mother:

Received your letter this morning. Should be home Saturday morning about 3:00 but might change my plans. Don't wait up for me just leave the door unlocked. Also received a telegram from Ed yesterday.

It was raining this morning and the temperature was about 45 (degrees), now it's almost 0 (degrees) and windier then the devil.

That's all until I return to Cooperstown.

Love

Rum

Thursday Feb. 19, 1943
Cooperstown, N.Y.

Dear Mother:

Received your letter this morning. As I haven't anything definite on my next location I held back on writing or calling.

This morning I received a letter from the draft board asking for a recommendation from someone in the Engineer Corp. I showed the letter to "Pop" Clark, the boss and he called the Colonel in New York to do something about it. The Colonel said he would send a telegram to the draft board immediately to get my release from the country. So I expect to go to Edmonton in about 5 or 6 weeks. I may be located somewheres from Edmonton to Alaska, as yet I haven't been assigned to any location. I'm going up there for a year at a salary of $3000 a year. One of the fellows is leaving this Tuesday. The route followed is from Buffalo to Toronto to Edmonton. It's just about a 4 day trip.

I'll probably stay in Cooperstown for a week or so. There's just 10 persons left in the office now and it sure is an empty looking place. I'll be in Buffalo for a couple of weeks before I leave for Edmonton. I'll need the time buying clothes, etc.

I received an offer from Pampa, Texas at the Advanced Twin Engine Flying School at $2000 a year but I turned it down.

It was cold in Cooperstown this past week. Monday morning the temperature was 34 (degrees) below zero. I wore my overcoat and ski cap but I froze one of my ears. It wasn't too bad tho but it did burn quite a bit and still does. Had dinner with Miss Christen Tuesday Evening. The girl who stays here was 21 years old and we celebrated her birthday.

There used to be 5 of us from the office staying here, now there's only 2. I received the box of candy you sent and also one from Mamie. It was very good especially the box you sent since there was a greater variety and more milk chocolate.

Received a letter from Ed yesterday. He said I should have gone to Atlanta, Georgia but that's not what I want.

I'm going to send my laundry home this weekend. Send it back unless I phone or write and tell you not to because I really don't know when I'll come home.

The ice carnival the Knox School girls put on last Friday was a marvelous sight. The rink is right across the street and we watched from the windows. Good thing too because it was below zero outdoors.

That'll be all for now and I might phone next week.

Love
Rum

Enroute to Edmonton
9:30 P.M. Eastern War Time
April 2, 1943

Dear Mother:

It got dark just about a half hour ago because we're getting so far west. In about 3 hours we shall get into the Central Time Zone. The train thus far is 3 hours late because of being sidetracked for passing freights.

I'm writing in the lounge car, on a desk but right now the train is wobbling and shaking to beat all heck.

We'll get into Winnepeg about 12:00 noon tomorrow. Will probably mail this letter from there.

There's nothing but wilderness around this country. Once in awhile we come across a logging camp or a couple of isolated cabins. There are no roads, electricity or the kind. It sure is a bleak looking civilization.

It was cold outdoors today, whether it was just a cold spell or ordinary weather, I don't know.

Expect to get into Edmonton some times Sunday afternoon.

The meals are quite steep and that $7.00 a day will be used up in 2 days.

I had 2 reservations when I got into Toronto. One was made in Utica and the other from Buffalo. None of the upper berths are taken. Right now I'm about 850 miles from home.

There are 2 Americans one from Utica and the other from Oneida. They are older fellows. One is a carpenter and the other is a laborer. They are going to work on the highway for a private contractor.

That's about all for now. Will send cards if possible.

Love

Rum

Wednesday April 7, 1943
7:30 P.M.
Edmonton, Alberta

Dear Mother:

Should have written sooner but just haven't been able to start. Arrived here Sunday at about noon. Went down to the main office where they also have rooms or barracks as you might call them. It's inconvenient but there are no rooms in town. I was also informed that I could stay in Edmonton and not be sent North. I don't care much for that. However the work is terrible and I dislike it as much as possible. I been seriously thinking of heading back home specially since I don't feel so well. On the whole everything is pretty bad.

Edmonton is full of people coming and going. Last night a bunch of fellows came from Alaska. Said it was 30 (degrees) below the morning they left. They flew down.

The office at which I work is downtown and I eat 2 meals there. At night I come to my room and have dinner at the mess hall which serves dinner at .50 in help yourself methods.

Fellow from Cooperstown was here Sunday when I arrived. He had been here for 2 weeks. However Monday Morning he left for the North Country.

Edmonton is a very large city and is quite difficult to get around until you become familiarized with the place.

When you send my mail please address it to U. S. Engineer Office, Edmonton Motors Building, Edmonton, Alberta, Canada.

It's been very warm here all week and haven't been wearing any topcoat. It gets sort of cool at night however. Plenty of sloppy mud where I'm staying at.

I believe I'll give this place a months' trial. If the type of work I do doesn't improve, and the conditions and mood I feel don't change I'll leave because I can't stand indoor work anymore.

There isn't much else to say. Edmonton is like any other city and that describes it entirely.

Right now its 10:00 P.M. where you are and here it is 8:00 P.M. and I'm writing this letter by daylight. Is Wally going into the Army?

Give my regards to all and goodbye.

Love
Rum

address:
U.S. Engineers
Edmonton District
Edmonton Motor Building
Edmonton, Alberta, Canada

Thursday, April 15, 1943
9:45 P.M.
Edmonton, Alberta

Dear Mother:

Received your 4 letters yesterday and today, 2 apiece, including the pictures. Still staying out at the college from which I'll have to move soon because they're rapidly making office out the sleeping rooms.

The set up in Edmonton is this way. There are 2 offices, one the Division and the other District. The Division provides rooms and meals. The rooms consist of apartment houses which have been built next to the office. Each apartment consists of 4 bedrooms and a large living room, with 2 persons to a bedroom, twin beds. The meals are served at the mess hall for civilians and military officers at .50 each. The food is excellent and plentiful, helping yourself to as much you want. However I'm not in the Division but District Office. Now the District Office is downtown and provides nothing, so I'll have to get a room in town and eat at restaurants. I rarely eat lunch because the restaurants are too crowded. Rooms are scarce so I'll have a tough time getting a descent room to sleep in.

The work down at the office is terrible because all the engineering work has been given to private contractors and what I have been doing would drive anybody nuts. I complained about the work several times and was promised to get something useful to do. Well several days passed and still no descent work. I complained again and was told there wasn't any work to do. This condition couldn't exist or can't exist so in about a week one of several things maybe done. First I may be transferred to the Division Office which I already explained about, second I may be transferred North and third I may be transferred back to the states. If one of the 3 doesn't happen I'll make my own move which would be to leave.

My laundry is being done by a woman who cleans the rooms and she charges .25 a shirt, .25 a pair of socks, etc.

Bonds or Victory Tax shall no longer be deducted from my check. Have you received my last check from New York or Cooperstown as I haven't gotten it as yet but have written to Cooperstown about it.

It was 76 (degrees) yesterday and seems more like the South then North Country. Don't bother sending me anything as I don't know how long I'll stay here.

In addressing me just put U. S. Engineer Office, Edmonton District, Edmonton, Alta, Canada. Shipping the Motor Building.

I'll send the pictures home sometime later. Some mail coming into the office is censored, but none of mine has been as yet. There's no one here I know except 3 girls from Massena. I went to a party they gave for the girl that returned from Alaska, about whom Ed sent the clipping. Guess I better quit because 2 sheets will be too heavy for airmail.

Love,

Rum

(Easter Card)

An Easter Rosary for You

A Rosary at Eastertime,
  Said quietly at heart,
With a prayer of tenderness and faith
  That you may have a part
In all the beauty of the day,
  Its peach and joy so true –
A Rosary at Eastertime,
  And offered just for you.

Saturday May 1, 1943
Edmonton, Alta, Canada

Dear Mother:

Received your 2 letters, one yesterday and another today.

I'm still working at the District Office however for the past 2 days I have been out in the field doing survey work and I really felt good for the first time since I been in Edmonton. It was sunny and windy all day and the fresh air was perfect. Got a nice burn and liked the work fine. It was the first time I did any surveying except for some I did in Potsdam about a year ago. I told them I had field work tho and was sent out. I got along allright too. We finished the job in 2 days and I was back in the office today. However there is more of that work coming up and a possibility of going North so I'll be contented with that thought in mind.

I'm still staying at the Division Office but still don't know if I can keep the room. Right now I'm in Unit 13, I was out my own socks because it takes too long for the laundry and they charge 6 cents a pair. Last time they lost 3 pair too. It's been quite cold lately and my lips became very chapped and dry while I was out in the field. I bought some camphor and that reduced the soreness quite a bit.

The days continue to get longer all the time. Right now the sun sets at 9:15 and it doesn't get dark till about 10:00.

Ed has sent me the last two issues of his army papers and his articles are quite good.

Received Adelines' letter in the past week also.

In the near future all Americans will have to use the Army Post Office and letters shall be censored because of the activities which are going on. I never mentioned anything of the war nature because of that reason and there is quite a bit to tell.

I'm very glad that you liked the roses. Do you wish my Canadian products such as a Hudson Bay Blanket or similar to that?

I believe that's about all there is to tell for now.

Love

Rum

Wednesday May 5, 1943
Edmonton, Alta, Canada

Dear Mother:

Just a short letter to send a check and money order. Got paid today and also received the check from New York which was for March. Also got a check for travelling from Buffalo to Edmonton today. The total receipts for the day was over $200.00.

Haven't gone out to the field anymore since I last wrote. There is still going to be a change made at the office but when or what is not known.

A fellow came down from Whitehorse today and I asked him about the two fellows that worked in Cooperstown with me. He knew them both and one is going back home to join the Navy Air Corps and the other expects to leave about June 1. They both don't care for the whole setup. There's only 4 of us here from Cooperstown, that is in the whole North Country. The 4th is up in the Northwest Territory. There were supposed to have been 2 more coming up but evidently they changed their minds because they never showed up.

It's been quite cool lately and rainy for the past couple of days. Received your last letter Monday.

I'm still staying out to the Division Office and evidently will be because no one seems to know I'm here.

That's all for now.

Love

Rum

P.S. – Do anything you wish with the money.

P.S. – Decided not to send check will make out money orders for it and mail it tomorrow or in the near future. Notice that the money order is made out for the Army Post Office in Seattle, Wash. We are suppose to use that address but it takes longer and all mail is censored when using that method. It isn't compulsory yet so I'll use the Canadian mail for the time being.

Technical Sgt. Edward F. Bartz
Company "A"
Academic Regiment, I.S.S.C.
Fort Benning, Georgia

MONDAY MORNING
11:30 O'CLOCK
JUNE 7TH, 1943

DEAR MOTHER:

JUST A FEW LINES. THIS IS MONDAY, WHICH IS ALWAYS BUSY. MEANT TO WRITE YESTERDAY, BUT IT WAS VERY HOT. ON SATURDAY THE OFFICIAL TEMPERATURE WAS 101 DEGREES. THAT'S IN THE SHADE. IN THE SUN IT WAS ABOUT 115. AM ENCLOSING A CLIPPING. YESTERDAY IT WAS MUCH HOTTER THAN SATURDAY, BUT HAVEN'T SEEN THE PAPER AS YET.

THIS MORNING I WILL SEND OUT A LITTLE BOX WITH MISCELLANEOUS ITEMS. INSPECTIONS HAVE BEEN A LITTLE MORE STRICT. SO I THREW SOME THINGS OUT AND AM SENDING SOME HOME. THE 2 INFANTRY SCHOOL PENCILS ARE FOR YOU, AS I GUESS YOU LOST THE OTHER ONE, DIDN'T YOU? I HAVE ANOTHER LAUNDRY BAG, SO AM RETURNING ONE. ALSO HAVE SOME OTHER POLO SHIRTS. ALSO RETURNING THE SMOKING PIPES AS I SAID I WOULD. PLEASE PUT THEM AWAY. SOMEDAY I'LL TAKE TIME TO ENJOY THEM BUT NOT DOWN IN THIS CLIMATE. I'M INSURING THE PACKAGE AS THE PIPES ALTOGETHER ARE WORTH $10.00.

SO LONG FOR NOW.

LOVE AND KISSES

Ed

(Article)
CAPTURE OF JAPS IN P. I. GOES ON

218 Killed, 73,600 Taken; Nips Ignorant of Peace

Manila (AP) – Two hundred and 18 Japanese soldiers have been slain in the Philippines since the war ended, with 67,000 soldiers and 6,600 civilians take prisoner from Aug. 20 to Oct. 23.

Western Pacific Army headquarters said many Japanese were so scattered it was difficult to reach them, while leaflets still are being dropped within 100 miles of Manila for Nipponese troops unaware that hostilities have ended.

Piedmont Hotel
Atlanta
Sunday
June 13, 1943

Dear Mother:

Arrived here yesterday at 5:30 pm, after leaving Columbus by bus at 1:30. I still prefer the train. I guess all the good bus drivers are in the army or in defense plants. The one we had yesterday couldn't get up Pine Mountain, and about 15 of us soldiers had to get out and walk about a quarter mile to the top, while he backed down and got another start. Then later he almost stripped the gears and the bus broke down at Warm Springs. One of the soldiers was a mechanic and he fixed it up after a half hour. Then the bus vibrated a bit.

Had a good time last night. The girl and I went to the Paradise Room in the Henry Grady Hotel. They had a good orchestra and a floor show. It was just like being in New York City.

This morning she and I went to Grant Park for a walk. Now I'm getting ready to catch the train back to camp.

Oh, yes, I was fortunate in getting a room here, right in center of downtown.

Tried to call you awhile ago, but there's a delay of 5 to 6 hours.

Well, so long for now.

Love & Kisses,

Ed

Tech. Sgt. Edward F. Bartz
Company "A" – Academic Regiment, I.S.S.C.
Fort Benning, GA.

Wednesday Afternoon
1415 o'clock

June 23, '43

Dear Mother:

Your Monday morning letter arrived this morning, which was pretty good service. Yes, it's still hot here, but we had a heavy rainstorm during the night which cooled it off for awhile. Anyway, it's some consolation that it won't get any hotter this summer than it has been (I hope).

Have you received any more of my War Bonds? Have you had any luck in getting a box or are just keeping them at home? By the way the Army has just made a ruling that every soldier has to take out $10,000. insurance or else sign a statement, giving a reason why he won't take it out. I had only $2,000. so today I took it out for $8,000. more as I had no good reason for not. Most of the fellows are doing the same. Incidentally it'll cost me $7.00 per month. I can always drop it if I wish.

Yes, the sight of paratroopers jumping from planes is something to see. Usually 12 of them jump out from each plane. It looks like popcorn popping up in the air. I think Helen Szewczyk's brother, Alex, is stationed here at the Post as a paratrooper as I saw something in the paper a while ago. Guess I'll have to look him up. Incidentally, the paratroopers get $50.00 extra per month in addition to their regular pay, so that a private gets $100.00 per month. They sure take a lot of risks. When I was in the hospital I saw quite a few of them with broken arms and legs; in another ward.

Am going to Atlanta this Saturday and tonight will send a telegram to the Piedmont Hotel for reservation as I found out that that's the best way to do it. They figure that if you take the trouble to telephone or telegraph, that you will really come. So many soldiers write in (which doesn't cost them anything) for reservations and then don't show up.

I haven't heard from Rum for just about a month. He really must not like to write. Do you know whether he works indoors or out?

I went swimming last night with Sgt. Daniel at the Russ Pool here on the post. Very nice, except that the water was too warm. It's fresh spring water too. It was the first time that I had gone swimming since January 2, 1942 while at the YMCA in New York City.   It's getting cloudy again and I hope it rains real hard. It gets quite tiresome seeing the sun shine day after day. Maybe at a beach it would be

different.
      So long for now.

                       Love and Kisses,

                       Ed

St. Joseph Church
Varysburg, N.Y.

Dear Friend, Mrs. Bartz,

Thank you very much for your favor. Assuring you that your generosity has been deeply appreciated, with sincerest best wishes to you and yours, hoping to see you soon, I remain, I have lighted the vigil candle. May God and Our Blessed Mother be ever with your dear son, Edward.

Fr. Lutz

Tech. Sgt. E. F. Bartz 32212187
Company "A"
Academic Regt. I.S.S.C.
Ft . Benning, Ga

Sunday
12:45 PM
June 27,'43

Dear Mother:

Arrived here yesterday at 5:30 pm. Had no difficulty in getting a room, as they already had one reserved for me. Last night the girlfriend and I went dancing at the Garden Terrace of the Biltmore Hotel. It's right out in the open and very nice. Haven't decided just what I'll do today. Have to leave at 6 pm on the train.

I suppose you've seen plenty of Georgia peaches on the market. They've been ripe for about 3 weeks down here. It's rather nice and cool here today, if you stay out of the sun.

I was going to call, but there's a delay posted so I gave up the idea.

So long for now.

Love & Kisses

Ed

Saturday
1355 o'clock
3 July 43

Dear Mother:

Well, here I am on duty this hot Saturday afternoon; not much to do but have to be here just the same. I put in for my furlough this morning, but of course as yet don't know how it's coming out. I asked for 12 days instead of 10, as I figure that what with traveling conditions being as they are at present I could use a little extra traveling time. I put in for July 20th thru August 1st. If it all works out the way I have planned, I'll leave here on July 19th at about 7:30 PM and arrive in Buffalo on July 21st at about noon. Butch's birthday is on the 22nd so I'll be there in time for it. I'm just hoping and praying that it'll be approved all around; I don't see any reason why it shouldn't. Will have to get someone to write my column for me for 2 weeks.

Can't think of anything else to write about right now so will say so long until the next time.

Love and Kisses

Ed

IMMEDIATE ACTION
IN REPLY
REFER TO WAR DEPARTMENT

Tuesday
1305 o'clock
6 July 43

Dear Mother:

Well, I've got the good news......my furlough has been approved and I should be home sometime on Wednesday July 21st. Of course, being in the Army there's always a chance of things being changed such as happened last summer when I was to go on a furlough.

But I guess everything will be alright. I'm also dropping a letter to Rum now and telling him that I expect to be home two weeks from now. In fact two weeks right from this minute I'll probably be near the state of Tennessee. Yes, they approved the 12 days. The Colonel said that anyone living way up on the Canadian border should get some extra time.

So long for now and I'll get some work done.

Love and Kisses

Ed

IMMEDIATE ACTION IN REPLY
REFER TO WAR DEPARTMENT

Wednesday
1540 o'clock
7 July 43

Dear Mother:

It sure is a hot day. Guess the temperature has gone over a 100 degrees. Well, anyway two weeks from now I'll be home where it'll be cooler. (I hope it'll be cooler anyway.)

I checked on the plane schedules and found that I could leave Atlanta at 7:00 am and arrive in Buffalo at 2:12 pm, only 7 hours later, The fare would be about $48.00 one way, which is quite a lot. I'll see yet as to what I'll do, but taking a plane would save one day and be less tiresome.

I'm going to send my Palm Beach uniform home by parcel post tomorrow. I'll address it to you and put a note to leave it downstairs if no one is at home at 497. Will you please have the suit dry cleaned and pressed. Another thing I'd like to have done is to have the shirt taken in at the sides about one inch on each side. It's a little too wide now. I guess you can have that done at the tailor at the same time while it's being cleaned & pressed.

I have several pair of shorts and undershirts at home, don't I? I won't bother taking any with me, except for the pair I wear. I want to carry as little as possible. I might even send one of my cotton uniforms later too.

So long for now.

Love and Kisses

Ed

Thursday
2245 o'clock
8 July 43

Dear Mother –

Lights will go out in 15 minutes, so I'll have to hurry along.

Your Monday letter came today. That sure was funny about Butch wondering why I want to go home as he thinks I'm on my vacation down here.

I sent out my Palm Beach uniform at noon today. Also put a note on the box to leave at 499 If you're not home.

I'll bet the time will just drag for me from now until I arrive home.

I'd better say goodnight for now.

Love & Kisses

Ed

Tuesday
1320 o'clock
13 July 43

Dear Mother:

Well, a week from now I should be on a plane only an hour away from Buffalo. I don't think I'll leave Columbus until on the midnight bus next Monday. Here's the reason: If I leave on the 8:30 PM bus and arrive in Atlanta at midnight, then I'd have to go to a hotel for the night. The airport is about 10 or 12 miles outside of Atlanta, and as my plane leaves at 7:00 am I'd have to get up quite early and rush around trying to get out there. So I'll leave here at midnight; then the Greyhound bus on which I'll be, goes pretty close to the airport and I'll get off there at about 4:30 AM. Maybe I'll be able to get some sleep before plane time.

I sent out my money order for $48.73 to the airlines yesterday via special delivery. So now I'm all set except wait for the day to come along.

It's too bad that there's gas rationing; if not then you probably could come out to the airport. Well, anyway I'll be home soon thereafter.

Well, so long for now and I'll see you in a week.

Love and Kisses,

Ed

R. E. Bartz
A. P. O. 722-D
Seattle, Wash.

Tuesday July 20, 1943

Dear Mother:

Long time since I last written. I suppose Ed came home today if all his plans worked accordingly. I hoped they did anyways. I believe I'll try to put in a phone call this coming Sunday. Since there is a difference of 2 hours in time it may be quite late, however it'll be sometime in the evening, maybe 11:00 or 12:00. I hope it doesn't disrupt any of your plans by staying home to wait for the call.

Received an interesting letter from Mamie today telling of her trip to the Beach with Wally and Butch. Butch must be getting to be quite the fellow now and pretty smart.

Did you hear the Vox Fox program last night? It originated from here and I was at the broadcast. You probably didn't listen since it isn't too interesting as a radio program but last night you might have enjoyed it.

Still playing ball in the evenings tho the mosquitoes still are getting the best of us. There are 3 army teams now and 2 civilian teams.

Work everyother Sunday as yet and will probably have to work all Sundays hereafter.

Believe I'll drop a line to Ed tonight too because he hasn't received a letter from me in a heck of a long time.

Combined with the fact that I don't care to write and interesting news is scarce I seldom take time to do so.

So Daniel is still around. Do you ever talk to him. He should have been in the army long before now. How's Freeman getting along nowadays?

So you thought I was in Detroit when you received my last letter. Wish I was. Just about a year ago I moved to Cooperstown, and you came just a little after that. It seems like no time at all since we were there.

The weather hasn't been too bad of late and the sun shines ever so often between damp spells.

Hope that you all have a pleasant 12 days during Ed's stay at home. Wish I could be there but there'll be another time.

Love

Rum

R. E. Bartz
Jesuit College
Edmonton, Canada

Saturday Sept 4, 1943

Dear Mother:

Letter of August 17 was the last time I heard from you. That's a long time tho it's hard to realize. Mamie has written a couple of times in the past weeks telling about her trip and vacation at the Beach. Also the general house moving that is going on with her and Adeline.

Things remain normal up here. Winter has already set in and its really cool these days and the snow is about ready to fly.

Received a notice from the draft board today. Deferred until February 23, 1944. Maybe I won't be home this year anymore. It's going on 6 months that I been here now.

Haven't heard from Ed in some time either. No one seems to bother to write anymore. It's my fault anyways for not writing back sooner.

Hope that everything is okay at home and maybe on Ed's next furlo I'll come home, to stay.

Tim Malakie and Joe Gandio are here. They expect to leave however, not caring very much for the whole set-up. The two are working down at the District where I started. I was there 2 months and 3 months here. I'm really ready for a change again tho its not likely. However I have some prospects on which I'm now working.

Maybe you're in Bradford now and haven't had time to write.

Goodbye for now and

Love

Rum

R. E. Bartz
A. P. O. 722-"D"
Seattle, Wash.
Tuesday Sept. 7, 1943

Dear Mother:

Just a short note to send this money order. Will send a longer letter
presently. Won another War Bond this afternoon. You may expect to get
it in the near future.
Plenty cool these days its real fall weather you'd expect in the latter part
of October.
Running out of info so I better quit because I'm working right now,
supposedly so anyways.

Love,

Rum

TECHNICAL SGT. EDWARD F. BARTZ
Company "A"
Academic Regiment, I.S.S.C.
Fort Benning, Georgia

Monday Eve
8:10 o'clock
11 October '43

Dear Mother –
Since the new general has arrived we're getting to be regular soldiers.
Yesterday morning we marched for two hours. I've been put in charge
of a platoon and give the orders for marching. I really enjoyed it, too,
even though I did get a couple of blisters on my feet. Starting today we
have to march to the school in formation and also back after work. I'm
in charge of the Infantry School detachment.
Yesterday we of Company "A" moved to another part of the barracks.
Mr. Sgt. Smith & I have a nice private room up on the <u>fourth</u> floor. Has
four windows, while the other one only had one. The stair climbing will
be real exercise.

Yes, I saw "Action in the North Atlantic" a couple of months
ago and thought it exciting.

Thanks for sending Bob's address. I'll write him one of these
days.

Goodnight for now.

Love & Kisses

Ed

Tech. Sgt. E. F. Bartz
Co. "D" 213th I. T. B.
66th Regt. I. R. T. C.
Camp Blanding, Fla.

Monday
25 Oct. 1943
8:10 o'clock

Dear Mother –
    Have just finished talking with you. The connection sure was
clear.
    We left Columbus last Thursday night at 11 o'clock. No, we
didn't get any Pullman car; in fact I think that the car in which we were
was from Civil War days. I guess I slept a couple of hours.
    We arrived in Jacksonville, Fla., at 8 A.M., and ate at a
restaurant there. Then left by train at 9:40 AM & got off at Starke,
where our barracks bags were already waiting for us. We carried them
to Army trucks, which took up to Camp Blanding. As I said over the
phone, there are no barracks, only wooden huts, but they're more
comfortable than tents anyway. It's more like being a soldier now. I've
been outside quite a lot & have a Florida suntan.
    We probably won't be assigned for about a week yet, but you can
write to me at the following address for the time being:
    Company "D"
    213th ITB
    66th Regiment, I.R.T.C.
    Camp Blanding, Florida
ITB stands for Infantry Training Battalion.
I.R.T.C. stands for Infantry Replacement Training Center
    Yes, the visit to St. Augustine yesterday was very interesting, as
you can tell from the folder I sent.
    Oh, yes, there's quite a large lake here at camp. I'm only a
quarter mile away from it. It's called Kingsley Lake. Very nice for
swimming. Not muddy like the river in Georgia.
    So long for now & I'll write more later.
                            Love & Kisses

                            Ed

UNITED STATES ARMY
Hq. Det. 217th Tng. Bn.
CAMP BLANDING, FLORIDA

Tuesday Evening
1900
9 Nov 43

Dear Mother:

I'm Charge of Quarters tonight, which means that I'm on duty here at Headquarters until 0800 tomorrow morning. No, it doesn't mean that I have to sit up all night. They have a cot here in the office and I bring my own mattress, blankets, etc. We all have to take turns at being here and it comes about once every nine days. That's in case something important should come up and also more or less to guard the place. When the turn comes on a Sunday it'll really make it a long day.

Your airmail letter, written last Friday nite and mailed on Saturday morning, arrive yesterday morning, so that wasn't bad service. Of course, Jacksonville isn't far from here and that's where the plane brings it.

Today the laundry case with uniforms, etc., which you sent, arrived. That really was quick too. Now I have a lot of clean summer uniforms, but as luck would have it, we're changing to woolen ones next Monday, as it has turned rather cold, and we've been wearing jackets for the past two days.

Yesterday, also I received a letter from Rum and only the second one since I was home on furlough in July. He mentioned about going home on leave and wondered when I would be able to go but of course, right now I can't very well tell.

You asked if I was near some town. Yes, Starke is only 7 miles from here and I'm now located only about 300 feet from the bus station. Up till I moved here I was about 5 miles from the station. Starke has a population of only about 5,000 people; two years ago it had only 1,400. In a way it reminds me of Massena, but of course the people aren't as friendly. It sure would be swell if I could make some civilian friends like I did in Massena, where I could go and visit, but I guess that isn't very possible as a soldier.

Yes, after I had sealed my airmail letter of a week ago, to you, I happened to think that I had forgotten to sign it and even mentioned it to Mamie.

Thanks a lot for the $5.00 bill which you enclosed. I think we're going to be paid tomorrow on a special payroll, for all of us. The fellows here in this battalion have come from various camps: Benning, Cp Fannin, Texas, Cp Robinson, Arkansas, Ft. McClellan, Ala., Ft. Bragg, N. C., etc.

Yes, I've really been rushed and it reminds me of when I started with the U. S. Engineers in Massena, three years on November 13th. Incidentally, yesterday was two years since I arrived in New York to work for the Engineers. Time sure flies.

Well, according to the papers it seems that the war in Europe will be over by next July. That sure will be good news. It can't come too soon.

I'm enclosing the bronze pin which I received from the Red Cross at Benning, for donating a pint of blood. Please save it for me.

Well, goodnight for now.

Love and Kisses

Ed

Sunday
14 Nov. 43
1705

Dear Mother –
    Spending the day here in Jacksonville. A couple of my friends and I came over this afternoon by bus.
    The city is really crowded with soldiers, sailors & marines. Have just been walking around and looking the place over.
    Received your Thursday morn letter, this morning. Yes, thanks for sending the army sweat shirt back. I wear it while sleeping and it feels comfortable.
    The cookies you sent arrived yesterday and hardly any were broken. Guess they handled it quite carefully. They're very good. Thanks.
    Then I'll say so long for now.

Love & Kisses

Ed

November 19, 43

Dear Mother: -

About ready to go bowling so will slash off a note.

Received a letter from Ed the other. He seems to like it somewhat but not as much as Benning.

Things around here are quiet and the weather warm. No skating or snow as yet tho it may happen any day now.

Received a package from Mamie today. Thank her for me please.

Expect to be home sometime before the 10th of December. Is there any room for me to stay?

Please don't send any packages or the such except mail.

About all for now –

Love

Rum

NOTICE OF CHANGE OF ADDRESS

Date   23 Nov. , 1943

This is to advise you that my correct address now is –

Tech. Sgt. Edward F. Bartz
Hq. Replacement & School Command / 1905 Sixth Ave., South
c/o Postmaster Birmingham 3, Alabama

Signature … Edward F. Bartz

Saturday Dec 4, 1943
4:00 P. M.

Dear Mother:
    Expect to leave tonight. Maybe by plane but most likely by train if I don't miss it.

    If I leave by train will be home sometimes Tuesday.

    Love

    Rum

Monday
9:30 PM
20 Dec. 43

Dear Mother –

Just finished addressing a few more Christmas cards and still have the red ink in the pen, but I'll use it anyway. So far I've sent out 46 cards, and have about 4 more to go. I'm enclosing a v-mail card from Mr. Blue, who went to Africa with the U. S. Engineers, when I was supposed to go. Rum knows him. Please save the greetings for me.

Received your card today, with $5.00. Thanks a lot. It'll come in handy. Also got $5.00 from the "O'Hara kids". Give them a kiss for me.

Well, the weather is back to normal again, which means it's quite warm. No coats needed. It sure was smoky last Saturday here in town. Am enclosing a clipping about it.

I feel almost as if I were living at home here. They really treat me nicely. I'm going to have Christmas Dinner here. Also have an invitation to a cocktail party next Sunday.

Received a letter from the Lieutenant and his wife at Benning, where I used to go once in awhile. They want me to spend the 2-day holiday with them. It would be nice to see some of my friends there at Benning, but I guess I won't be able to make it because of the other invitations. Benning is about 165 miles from here. Takes about 6 hours by train. Up north you could almost go from Buffalo to N. Y. in that time. Incidentally, the train on which I came from Florida was a streamliner, which goes from Miami to Chicago, thru Birmingham.

I've received gifts from the O'Hara's, Gostylas, O'Hara kids, Mary, Peggy, Mrs. Johnson, Irene Gosulewski and you. It'll be nice to open them up on Christmas. The package you sent here to the house came on Saturday.

I might call on Christmas Day if the lines aren't too busy. Still don't know whether Rum is coming or not. Why don't you come down too? There's room for you here too. It would be nice.

I was going to buy some liquor today, to have for the party here. The line at the store was over a block long and didn't seem to move at all. I stayed for over a half hour & then left. Will try later in the week. They get recent shipments in on Sunday and so Monday is always so busy.

So long for now and Merry Christmas.

Love & Kisses

Ed

Friday
21 January 44
8:40 P. M. C. W. T.

Dear Mother –

I've had invitations to dinner almost every night this week and therefore haven't been home here long enough to write. Incidentally, I now have breakfast and supper here at the house, which makes it very nice. She charges me $15.00 a month for that and $15.00 for the room, so $30.00 per month isn't bad at all.

As I told you over the phone on Wednesday, this Lt. & his wife came from Benning for a 3-day visit in B'ham. They had had me in for dinner so often at Columbus, so I thought I'd repay them, and it turned out the other way. They insisted on paying for my dinner and later we went to see "Lassie Come Home" which I enjoyed very much.

Thanks again for the fruit cake. I'm enclosing the three post marks from the package, which will show how quickly it traveled. Thursday night, Buffalo; Friday night, Cincinnati & Saturday night, B'ham.

Well, I spoke about my furlough to Capt. Ash yesterday and he didn't seem to be happy about my going. He said he'd think it over. You see, there's no one who really could do my work, without a lot of instructions. However, I'm going to keep after him. After all if the captains and majors, can get leave, I a lowly Tech. Sgt., should be able to. I'll know definitely in a few days.

"As Thousands Cheer" hasn't been here as yet, but I'll go to see it when it does.

Incidentally, remember last summer, just after my return from furlough, I wrote that I had seen Ronald Colman and Greer Garson in "Raudner Haroist" and that it was the best movie I had seen in a couple of years? Well, you've probably read that it has been picked as the best picture of 1943. They're going to show it again here in B'ham, and I'm going to see it again. No doubt, they will show it in Buffalo too.

Well, the magazines have finally got my address straight again. My copies of TIME, YANK and Readers Digest were going to Benning & Blanding. I still haven't received any copies of LIFE. Guess it takes a little time.

Well, tomorrow marks two months that I've been here. It seems much longer than that, because I know so many people here. It seems like when I lived in Massena.

Goodnight for now. Hope to see you soon. Incidentally, I was home just a year ago today, after leaving the hospital.

Love & Kisses
Ed

505—NTS—Sampson—7-14-43----60M

Date 2-3-44

I have arrived at the Naval Training Station.
My address is:

D-16- Upper
Company No. 233
U.S. Naval Training Station
Sampson, New York

(Do not use nickname)

(Unsigned from Roman)

2-3-44

Dear Mother –

Dropping a line to let you know my address. It's 7:30 A.M. now and we've been up for 2 hours already.

Yesterday was quite a tough day – from 5:30 in the morning to 9:30 in the evening –

But everyone has to go thru it and it isn't so bad –

Rum

R. E. Bartz; A. 5.
Co. 233; Upper D-16
U.S. Naval Training Station

Sampson, New York
2-3-44
6:30 – Evening

Dear Mother –
Well here is the first letter I've had a chance to write. I just bought this stationary too – first chance to get that too.

Got here Tuesday at 1:00 o'clock in the afternoon. Had another physical exam, a couple of shots in the arm and then fitted out with clothes. The bag in which it came in was over 6 feet long. Wednesday we got up at 5:30 in the morning and worked pretty hard stenciling our uniforms. To bed at 9:30 in the evening.

Today was an easy day tho. All we did was some marching. Went to a lecture, then to a movie on war subjects.

Tonight however I'm the dormitory guard and will have to stay up till 12:00 midnight. However that's not bad because the next guy has to guard from 12:00 to 4:00 in the morning.

I find the whole thing quite interesting. This thing is called a "boot" camp and we wear boots or leggings during our entire training. A guy can become pretty well toughened up here in no time.

According to present plans, that is if they aren't changed, the training will last for 5 weeks. Then we get a 3 week furlough. That would be pretty nice.

Is Ed enjoying his furlo. It seems like ages that I've been home. That's all and love

Rum

U.S. NAVAL TRAINING STATION
SAMPSON, NEW YORK

My Dear Madam or Sir:

We are happy to inform you that a member of your family has reported to this station to begin training for the United States Navy. The Navy has gladly accepted the responsibility for his welfare and security.

When a man enlists in the Navy, he is assigned to a Naval Training Station for fundamental recruit training. During this period, the Navy endeavors to produce a future leader of men, a man of whom his family, his community, and the Service will be proud. The Navy guarantees you that the recruit will receive the best medical and dental care possible, and his mental and moral welfare is assured. Religious counsel and opportunities for public worship are ever present. Men of all faiths are under the constant supervision of the Chaplain Corps, and services are conducted on the Station weekly.

The first twenty-one days at the Training Station are spent in detention, which is necessary as a health measure. Good health, a Navy tradition, is furthered by prohibiting visitors during the detention period, thereby guarding against the spread of contagious diseases.

While visiting is not prohibited after this detention period, it is restricted. Your attention is particularly invited to the total lack of hotel and restaurant accommodations, as well as transportation facilities in this vicinity. Recruits are here but a comparatively short period, and will ordinarily be granted leave at the end of their recruit training. You can save rubber, oil and gasoline, or space on a train vitally needed for troop movements, thereby contributing your part to the national war effort, by remaining at home with positive assurance that he is busy, healthy and happy.

If unusual circumstances indicate the necessity of visiting a member of the family at this Station, it will be necessary to have him request a pass, which he will mail to you. Each pass is good for the date specified only. Since visiting is restricted to immediate members of the family, this pass is necessary to identify you as an authorized visitor. Visiting under these conditions is limited to Sundays from 1:00 P. M. until 4:30 P. M. Patients at the Naval Hospital may receive visitors on Wednesday, Saturday and Sunday between 2:00 P. M. and 4:00 P. M.

Cheerful letters from home are of real benefit to the recruit, and are the best means of encouraging him to correspond frequently. Although the recruit is instructed to write home often, he sometimes fails to do so. This should not be cause for alarm, however, for you will be notified immediately in case of serious illness. Letters addressed to him at Upper D-16 CO-235 "U.S. Naval Training Station, Sampson, New York, Company " will be delivered promptly to him while he is in training. You should instruct him to keep you informed of any change in his address, so that his incoming mail may not be delayed.

In the event of serious emergencies arising at home, the recruit should be notified by telegraph, preferably through your local Red Cross Chapter, as incoming telephone lines are required for official use. If a return call is requested public telephones are available.

Inquiries regarding recruits should be addressed to the Recruit Training Officer, U.S. Naval Training Station, Sampson, New York.

Sincerely yours,
H. A. BADT, Captain, U.S.N., Commandant.

"If YOU COULD ONLY SEE THE BOYS IN CAMP"

"If you could see them just once—lined up each night to telephone home—you wouldn't make another unnecessary call as long as this war lasts.

"For your unnecessary call may be the one that ties up a line and keeps their calls from going through.

"Remember—there are only so many Long Distance circuits and no way to build more.

"So please try not to use Long Distance in the only hours most boys are off —between 7 and 10 o'clock at night."

NEW YORK TELEPHONE COMPANY

U.S. Naval Training Station
Sampson, New York

2-5-44
7:00 P. M.

Dear Mother –
Today was a very easy day and things aren't so bad as they first appeared.

Last night's telephone call was about 10 minutes but because it came from Sampson the operator let us talk because just as I was about to hang up she said 3 minutes were up while actually it was closer to 10 minutes.

I received a letter from Ed today which he wrote yesterday just before I called I guess.

Got paid today (10 dollars) and also received our haircuts. They sure cut it short.

We do our own washing, our equipment is swell. Two white woolen blankets, 6 uniforms and a stack of other stuff.

Tomorrow Sunday we don't do anything except go to church. Monday we take our swimming tests. Tell Milton not to go to the Navy if he doesn't like the water because you have to learn or you don't get out of "boot" training.

We are located right smack on Seneca Lake and 12 miles South of Geneva. Still have 2 ½ hours before lights out and anything we wish to do.

That's about all I have to relate –

Love

Rum

U.S.Naval Training Station
Samson, New York
2-9-44 5:00 P. M.

Dear Mother –

Just had "mail call" and received letters from you, Adeline and Mamie. I won't be able to write them because there isn't much time to do so. Anyhow they can read this.

Sunday we rested all day. Listening to the radio, playing cards. However I had guard duty from 9:30 P. M. to 1:30 in the morning outside. It wasn't bad however. There were 2 of us and we had on heavy artic coats over our regular coats.

Monday we took our swimming tests which I naturally passed. In the afternoon we took our classification tests. Yesterday we were classified. If a fellow had low marks they send him on a ship to swab desks and do the dirty work. Others who obtain good marks are sent to school. The Navy shall try and place me as a draftsman so they are going to write to Washington to see if there are any vacancies. If not I'll become a radio technician or an electrician's mate for which they will send me to school for. I couldn't become an officer because I'm not a college graduate.

I sent my shoes home this morning because we had our others fixed with extra soles and heels.

Today we had our double typhoid shots. The arms around here are plenty sore too and most everyone is complaining. Mine isn't so bad.

Received a card from Ed which he sent from New York.

It's plenty cold around here because of the wind coming off the lake. However there is no snow at all. We do plenty of drilling and exercising and it's probably doing me plenty good. We also have lectures and education movies during the day. Last night there were boxing matches and proved very good. Tonight there's a movie on themes enough to do in fact too much.

That's all because soon we'll be heading for class.

Love

Rum

U.S. Naval Training Station
Sampson, New York
2-12-44
6:00 P. M.

Dear Mother –

Receive a letter from you just about everyday. Tho I like to receive them don't trouble yourself in writing so often.

It started snowing last night and is still going quite strong. It's plenty deep and colder than the devil. Today, Saturday and Sunday we don't have much to do but rest and it sort of comes in handy. This morning I took my radio technicians test. If I passed, I'll go to school for 9 months. The course costs the Navy $11,000 to instruct one person. At the end of 9 months those who have passed become petty officers 1st class which is equivalent to a first sergeant in the Army.

Received your valentine today. Also one from Mamie. One from Adeline yesterday. Also received the pictures you sent. They came out quite well.

According to present plans I'll be home March 3rd which is just about 3 weeks away. Did you hear from the jeweler yet? Don't send the watch however because the one I have is alright for now. Received a card from Al. What is his address? I've forgotten it.

How did Sonny make out with the draft board?

About all for now.

Love

Rum

Thursday
8:35 P.M.
17 Feb. '44

Dear Mother –

Received your Monday night letter today. That phone bill sure was high, but the dates sound alright. I only called once when I didn't reverse the charges and that was in December. I called on the 9, 19, 24 and then you called on the 25th.

Yes, I have the slippers that Rum brought from Edmonton and wear them every day.

So Ronnie is home. I just wrote to him a week ago. Wonder if he'll get the letter. If you see him tell him "hello" for me.

So Rum is writing quite often. One reason I suppose is that he has something to write about. I wonder whether he'll come down here on his furlough.

No, I haven't been too busy lately but several things will happen to make us busy in a few days. A few changes in our set-up.

Oh, incidentally, they decided I should get the additional pay for my 3 years at the 107th F.A., and so I'll get it month after next, plus for the past 3 months, about $15.00. I got a brand new pair of Army shoes yesterday, as the old ones could not be repaired.

It really is warm here today, about 70°, and raining.

Well, I guess I'll say goodnight for now with

Love & Kisses

Ed

U. S. Naval Training Station
Sampson, New York
2-17-44
7:30 A.M.

Dear Mother –

Just came back from breakfast. Have been up for 2 hours already. Getting up so early makes the day so long and the 17 days I've spent here have been the longest ones in my life.

It has been very cold here for the past few days but this morning its not windy and quite warm.

The same things continue to happen, going to lectures, etc. Today we are going to have rifle range.

Had another shot in the arm yesterday and there's only 2 more to go. Had 4 so far.

Had other group picture taken last night in our blues.

We won't have much to do for another hour or so.

So Ronny is back home. Where was he anyways? Will you get me his address?

My hair is growing back slowly but still is quite short.

Received a letter from you everyday so far. Also got one from Ed the other day. Mamie has sent a couple and so has Adeline.

Nothing else but –

Love

Rum

U. S. Naval Training Station
Sampson, New York
Sunday 8:00 A.M.
2-20-44

Dear Mother –

Slept till 6:00 this morning. Just back from breakfast, going to church at 10:00.

They changed the time of our training and added on 5 more days. It might change again so don't depend on mine coming home on a certain date, as it is now we leave March 8th and get 2 weeks leave but it easily can be March 15th and only one week leave. It is all up to the number of men that are coming in. Great Lakes Naval Training Station is now open which will make this place ass crowded.

It warmed up quite a bit today and yesterday. The worse part is when the wind is blowing off the lake.

The whole thing is almost routine now. Tuesday our company (112 men) take over the mess hall so that will be different. We will have it for a week and during that time we shall have no lectures and stuff like that.

Received a letter from Sonny the other day.

There isn't much more.

Love

Rum

U. S. Naval Training Station
Sampson, New York
2-22-44
6:30 P.M.

Dear Mother –

Well I'm still going after 3 weeks. The weather has warmed up a bit hasn't been so bad. When its cold and windy it makes things so much more miserable.

We are finished with all of our training, most of it anyways. We just do odd jobs around the place. We chopped ice all this morning. I don't think we will get any kitchen work however and that's a break because that is about the worse job around here.

Yesterday we received our second harircuts. It was just a slight trimming of the sides and back this time.

This afternoon we didn't do a thing so it was pretty easy.

Had an injection for yellow fever Monday. That made the 5th shot, only one more to go.

Everyone who had defective teeth had to go to the dentist. Quite a few fellows had about 4 or 5 pulled and they were quite miserable. I didn't even have to go so I had a break there.

We still are to leave March 8 but as I said it might change and we will have to stay here longer.

Received a letter from Miss Chicslin and she said I should remember her to you, Adeline and Butch. She isn't staying at her place anymore but working at the old peoples home.

That's about all –

Love

Rum

U.S. Naval Training Station
Sampson , New York
Saturday 2-26-44
6:00 P. M.

Dear Mother –

Another week has ended. It wasn't too bad. We worked 2 days in the mess hall cleaning grills, etc. Today we did hardly anything. There are ways of getting out of doing all the dirty work and we have been using them all.

It has been swell so far as weather is concerned for the past week. Today it got cold and windy again. Some rain too but not much.

Going to a movie tonight. Last Sunday went to a couple of radio broadcasts. One to Rochester and the other to Syracuse.

Received our last injection and that sure is a relief. My arm looks like a punch board and is sore right now.

Going to be usher at church tomorrow.

I don't need any money. Haven't spent more than 5 dollars since I have been here and that's 4 weeks. A dollar a week is pretty economical.

After Tuesday I guess we start doing manual arms. That is practicing with rifles for parades and stuff like that.

Got our dog tags 2 of them. That's about all the things that have happened during the past couple of days.

Love

Rum

Wednesday
2135
1 March '44

Dear Mother –

Just a few words and am enclosing pictures I had taken here. Also a clipping from the Sunday paper. When you finish showing the snapshots you might as well keep them for me as I have the negatives. The girl is Mary Bevans, daughter of the landlady. Next time I hope to get some snapshots of the girlfriend.

The year sure seems to be going by fast. Here it's March already.

Last night, Beth & I went to see the play "Junior Miss" and really enjoyed it.

Well goodnight for now.

Love & Kisses

Ed

U. S. Naval Training Station
Sampson, New York
Wednesday
8:00 P. M.

Dear Mother –
 Still here and may not go out this week. If I do stay I'll be
home Saturday morning about 10 o'clock. Must be back here Monday
morning at 6:00.
 Been pretty cold lately and rainy. Not doing much but reading
around the barracks. No guard duty or anything. Theres only about 10
men left from my company. I don't know what they are going to do with
me because the radio technicians are going out tomorrow. Maybe they'll
still make me a draftsman.
 Hope to see your Saturday –

Love

Rum

P.S. Don't depend on mine coming home too much because something
may happen between now and Saturday. If my name shows up
tomorrow I will leave Saturday for someplace.

U. S. Naval Training Station
Sampson, New York

March 22, 1944
6:30 P. M.

Dear Mother —
Well my second day is almost done since I returned. We arrived
about 2:00 yesterday and sat around in the drill hall till 7:00 in the
evening. Then some barracks were vacated by another group of men
and we moved in. So at least we have a place to sleep.

Didn't do a thing today. Slept all afternoon and just about
caught up with my sleep.

About 20 fellows from my company are leaving tomorrow.
I don't know as yet what is to happen to me. There is quite a bit of
confusion here and it isn't much fun. I haven't unpacked. Just left my
stuff in the sea bag and ready to go most anytime.

It is sort of tough coming back after being home 2 weeks but
that will pass over.

You can send mail to this address and if I move before it comes
it will be forwarded. I might leave at anytime and I could stay for 2
weeks, can't tell. Don't send the pictures here however.

Love

Rum

U. S. Naval Training Station
Sampson, New York
Sunday – March 26, 1944
10:00 A. M.

Dear Mother –

Well I'm still around not doing much of anything but just waiting. My name hasn't shown up on the list as yet for those who are to leave. Out of 100 men in my company at least 70 are already gone. Maybe I'll get that Radio Technician School because one starts on the 15th of April. Will go to Chicago for 4 weeks if I do.

If I'm here this weekend I might be able to come home but that is quite problematical. Sleep as late as you want to around here and I'm getting plenty of sleep. Got up at 9:00 this morning which gave me more sleep then I ever got at home while on leave.

I'm still brushing Duchess out of my clothes.

The weather has been perfect around here for the past couple of days.

Hope the kids are feeling better especially Donnie. He sure was acting up the day I left. How is Adeline's throat?

It seems as tho I always go to some new place around April 1st. Last year Edmonton, 3 years ago Massena and this year someplace else.

Received a letter from Mamie which she send to the old barracks. Got it right away too.

Tuesday a new bunch comes in so probably we will have to move out of these barracks.

When I do leave I won't know where I am going till I'm on the train so I won't be able to show you and tell you. I might phone anyways. Maybe today.

There's no more to write –

Love

Rum

Wednesday
9:30 PM
5 April 44

Dear Mother –

Have received the pipes OK. Thanks. I'm smoking one of them right now.

Just got this stationery, as I needed some and liked the looks of this, but it's a little too rough. Like sandpaper.

Thanks for the information about having my watch checked. I'll send it one of these days.

Am enclosing $75.00 money order. Wish you would take some of it for yourself and not put it all in the bank for me. Get yourself some new clothes. I put $50.00 in the bank here this pay day, just to have some handy.

Well, Rum has been back at Sampson for two weeks now. He should be getting reassigned soon. Yes, I remember when Rum went to Massena on April 1st, 3 years ago. Time sure has gone by fast.

It's been quite cold here lately. Seems strange, here's it's April & way down South, and yesterday we had frost. All the rooftops were white in the morning.

Really am busy at the office. On Monday I worked until 10 PM.

Well, goodnight for now.

Love & Kisses

Ed

Roman E. Bartz; 512C
HYDROGRAPHIC OFFICE
U.S. NAVY
WASHINGTON, (25) D.C.
c/o AIR NAVIGATION ROOM 238

April 6 –
1:00 P. M.

Dear Mother –
Well here I am in Washington and things are coming out quite good.

Left Sampson Tuesday morning. It was a nice day too. Got into Philadelphia at 9:00 P. M. that night and it was cold and raining. We had a couple of beers there and got a train for Washington. Into Washington at 12:00 midnight. I was quite tired and no one seemed to know the place where I was suppose to report. I finally went to the Navy Yard and they gave me a place to sleep.

Next morning I went to the Naval Barracks where I was suppose to have gone. It's good I didn't tho because there are all Wave Barracks and I couldn't have stayed there anyways.

I ran all around Washington to places I had to go to. It sure was tough not knowing the streets and places I was to go. I finally got straightened out however. I went down to the office this morning and was acquainted with the people I'm to work with. I'm to work from 5 in the afternoon to midnight. The rest of the time is mine so with summer coming on I can get plenty of the outdoors and it gets plenty hot here too.

I'm not living in any barracks but in a private home. It's not a very good place but I grabbed the first thing and will find something better after I get to know the town. I live in Maryland and also work out there. It's about 5 miles from Washington. I'm getting $3.05 a day for living expenses. I went to the red cross and borrowed $50.00 because I only had 10 dollars. I didn't think that I would get a job like that. So Ed and I are both living like civilians now.

I'm going to do drafting work and eventually get a specialists rating which is one of the best to get in the Navy. I was also told that I could apply for a commission after being here awhile.

I came here on temporary duty but the work I'm going to do has the highest priority of anything and might stay here for the duration.

They don't take men here under 30 years old but because of my experience and college they accepted me.

You ought to see the waves around here. There any number of them. The women here outnumber the men 10 to 1.

There's only one thing I don't like and that's the place where I stay but I'll move out as soon as possible.

The cherry blossoms are already out but it has been very cold and windy. Just like Buffalo.

Washington itself is the nicest large city I have ever been in. The buildings are something to see. Seen the White House, Capitol and many other places already.

That's about all for now except that I won't be able to get home for awhile. We work 6 days a week. In about a month I'll be able to get every other weekend off that means Saturday and Sunday.

I'll probably try and see Ed if he can meet me half-ways some weekend. I don't know how far it is but if he traveled about 300 and myself 300 I think that would just about make it. Well that's all and I hope that everything is okay at home.

Love

Rum

USO

April 8, 1944

Dear Mother —

Sorry that I didn't get a chance to send you an Easter Card but I have been quite busy that I just didn't have a chance to do so.

It's very hot down here and I bet the summer will really be a dandy. I found myself a new place to live and will move tomorrow.

I like the place quite a lot. I do drafting work as I did before and the office I work in is new and working conditions are fine.

Today being Sunday I don't have to work. Just work 8 hours a day 6 days a week. Get every other weekend off too so it's pretty soft.

I might try and make it home. It takes 12 hours to get home though and I don't know if I could get the trains at the right time.

I'll give you my address where I stay next time and if you don't mind sending a couple of pair of pajamas, 6 pair of socks from Tom MacMan size 11 ½ and a jar of that shaving lotion I would like to have it.

That's about all I need. Maybe later on I could have my camera sent. Maybe I'll get a chance to come home though and take it back myself.

Hope that you had a Happy Easter. I'll see if I can get a phone call through now. If it takes too long I won't bother.

Love
Rum

Saturday Afternoon

12:40 o'clock

15 April 44

Dear Mother:

Am very busy here at the office, but just wanted to drop you a few lines and ask whether you would send me the Palm Beach summer uniform, which I sent home last year. We're going to change to our summer uniforms on May 1st and I'm sure I'll be able to wear that uniform. I realize that one of the pockets is torn off on it, but I should be able to get it fixed.

Last night Beth & I went to the Oscar Levant piano concert and enjoyed it very much. We're going to the Ice Revels next Tuesday night.

Guess I'd better close and get back to work, if I want to get off at 5:00 o'clock tonight, which I do.

Love & Kisses

Ed

Friday 3:00 P. M.

Dear Mother –

Received your letter with 2 dollars and also others with a dollar in them. You needn't send anymore because I got paid Wednesday. Received $102.00 dollars so that will keep me going for awhile. Also received your package with pajamas, cigarets, etc. Thank you for everything. I'll have enough socks for now so don't send anymore. One pair of pajamas ripped already but 2 will be enough. Navy laundry takes only 5 days at the most.

Most of the Easter eggs were cracked. The other sailor that stays here and I ate most of them. However 2 cracked ones smelled rotten so I threw them out.

Received the Easter Card you sent to Sampson. Also one from Al which he sent there. It came yesterday – 2 weeks to catch up with me.

Takes 12 hours to get home by train. Leave here about 8 and get into Buffalo 8 Saturday night. Would have to leave Buffalo 10 Sunday night and get back to Washington about 10 Monday morning.

It's only 3 hours ride to New York and I might go there on a weekend. Haven't been there since 1941.

Been pretty rainy lately. Gets warm but then comes the rain and it becomes cool.

Received the peanuts Mamie sent. The waves ate most of them up as I opened them up at the office.

That's all for now –

Love

Rum

Sunday April 23, 1944

Dear Mother –

Just like winter here today. Damp and cold and a drizzling rain. So far the weather has been anything but good.

We finally got some new drafting tables and a room in the office. Now that we have our own equipment we'll change to the day shift. We start tomorrow at 8:30 A. M. to 5:00 P. M. Working on the night shift gave me plenty of sleep but that's about all I did besides work.

I tried to get some undershirts (skivvies we call them) at the Navy Supply Store but they didn't have my size. At the commercial stores the shirts cost 65 cents while at the Navy Store only 35 cents. I wonder if you have any at your store. I wear size 36 and would need shorts to go with them, white of course because any other color would show thru the white uniforms which we shall be wearing soon. I would need about 4 sets. Don't get them however if the shirts are more than 35 cents because I might be able to get them later on.

Received your box of candy yesterday. They were or are very good. The cherry one got smashed tho and the whole box was awful sticky but that was the only one the others were in good shape.

Received Adeline's Service Card yesterday too. What's the idea of sending those? Maybe because I neglect to send cards out for birthdays, Easter, etc. and in that way it's a good reminder.

Incidentally David should be in England or Italy by now as the last time I heard he was in the water going across.

Haven't written to Sonny as yet.

The Secretary of the Navy is coming up to see us tomorrow. He's coming to the office anyways. We probably won't even see him.

Washington certainly has some beautiful buildings. If it wasn't so crowded you could take a trip down here. Reservations can be made at any hotel a week in advance however and should you decide to come I'll make arrangements.

There isn't anything more for now.

Love

Rum

P.S. If you should ever want to call me the phone number is TRINADAD 7061 (Mrs Lee owner) Wash. D.C.

Thursday
27 April 44
6:30 P. M.

Dear Mother —
Guess I'm getting a little behind in my correspondence to you. Believe I've received two letters from you since I last wrote.

I've received two letters from Rum since he's been in Washington and have answered both of them.

I'm going to send my wristwatch home tomorrow. I hope it can be fixed in a week.

I'm enclosing a couple of new photos, which I had taken, with my new chevrons. I knew you won't care very much for one of them as I have my new cap on and look too serious.

Will return your snapshots under separate cover, unless, I can squeeze them in with my photos after I finish this letter. I'm keeping some of them.

Went to the Ice Show last Tuesday and it was really good. Enjoyable music and colorful costumes and good skating.

The mail service has been quite good lately. You mentioned that you received one of my Saturday afternoon letters on Monday. You wrote a letter on Tuesday afternoon, it was postmarked 6:00 PM, and I received it on Thursday morning.

Thanks for sending my Palm Beach uniform. I don't what I'll do about the pocket yet. Incidentally I've got a brand new pair of Army shoes and 2 new summer shirts. The old items wore out and I turned them in. Guess it's about time, as I've had the stuff for over 2 years now.

I've really been busy lately but am not working nights or Sundays, and get Friday afternoons off. Then I usually go to the YMCA for a soiree.

I wrote to Rum and gave him Beth's address in New York, so he can look her up there. If he wants to be sure to have a place to stay, should wire for a reservation.

Well, it looks as if the invasion in Europe will begin in a few weeks now. It's really going to be something.

I'm going on a wiener roast this Saturday night which should be fun.

Well, I guess that'll be all for now. So long.

Love & Kisses

Ed

Sunday
14 May 44
11:55 P. M.

Dear Mother –

    Put in a phone call to home at noon today, but it hadn't come through by 2:30 so I cancelled it, as Beth & I were going bicycling. She has her own bicycle and I used her brother's, who's in the Army. We sure had a lot of fun and exercise. It's been a beautiful day and I got quite a sunburn. The temperature was about 80°. We went out in the country for awhile. Came back home just at sunset. Then had a good meal at her home and then played records, mostly Tschaikowsky. Played "1812 Overture"; "Marche Slave", "Nutcracker Suite", "Piano Concerto", and "Romeo & Juliet".

    Yesterday at the office I was told that I would leave here about June 30th, which is longer than I expected. Of course, that may be changed. I'm going to ask for a furlough next month. Even now with the new sergeant, we're still busy all the while. He said he wondered how I did it alone; also he's wondering how he'll do it, after I leave.

    Well, Captain Ash leaves tomorrow afternoon for his new assignment in Washington, D. C. He invited me to visit him at his apartment last Thursday evening. We had a nice long chat about all our experiences during the past two years we've been together. He's going to see what kind of assignment he can get for me when he gets to Washington.

    It's nice that Rum can come home every other weekend, if he wants to.

    Well, it's after midnight and I'm a little tired from the bike ride, so I'll say goodnight.

Love & Kisses

Ed

Monday
8:15 PM
15 May 44

Dear Mother –

Received your Thursday evening letter today.

Well, Capt. Ash left for his new assignment in Washington this afternoon. He came in to say goodbye to me.

The reason I'm being transferred is that there's a War Department regulation which states that all soldiers who have been in an overhead installation for a year or more and are not limited service, have to be assigned to a field unit. Of course, both of my assignments, at the Infantry School and here have been called "overhead" installation. Now I'll probably be assigned to a Division. For that reason I guess I won't be able to get an assignment in Washington, D.C. but Capt Ash will try he said. That sure would be something if Rum and I were in Washington at the same time.

Just reading in the local paper that the high temperature here in B'ham yesterday was 93°, and we were out bicycling.

The girlfriend made me about 2 pounds of fudge. It really is good.

I had a toothache, and so went to the dental clinic out at the Army Air Base. It was a slight cavity and they fixed it up; also fixed another tooth. It's the first time I've been to an Army dentist and it wasn't bad at all. They tell me to come back to have them cleaned.

I felt a little sore today after all that bicycling yesterday. Beth did too. Did I tell you that we always walk home together? She works downtown and meets me at the hospital where I work. It's about a mile and a half walk for her and a mile for me.

Well, guess I'll close now and say goodnight.

Love & Kisses

Ed

May 16, 1944
8:30 P. M.

Dear Mother –

About time I wrote. Don't seem to get a chance to do so very much since I've been working days.

Got bck to Washington alright that Sunday. Rode back with a fellow from East High who is also in the Navy. He is stationed 60 miles from here however. Brought him up to the house to clean up then I showed him some of Washington. Saturday I went to Maryland about 30 miles from D.C. and stayed overnight at a friend's house. Sunday we went down to West Virginia. Passed thru Harper's Ferry where John Brown made history just before the Civil War. Had a homemade chicken dinner too down here. It was a pretty good weekend. This coming weekend is my regular weekend off. Haven't decided what to do yet tho I might go to New York.

We put on our white uniforms yesterday. They are cool but get dirty very fast. Have to change every other day. The weather has been so hot lately tho that I'm glad to wear them.

A sailor who stays at the same place I stay got me 5 pairs of shorts and shirts today at the Navy Store so I have enough now. Now I only have to get some more white uniforms and I'll be all set for awhile.

Played ball last night and bowled tonight.

There isn't much more that I have done. Received the slippers.

Love

Rum

Monday
7:40 P. M.
22 May 44

Dear Mother –

Received your Saturday morning letter today, which was pretty good service.

I asked whether I could have Saturday afternoons off instead of Friday and I guess I'll get them alright. Had last Saturday PM off and Beth and I went out bicycling again.

Received a letter from DiPasquale yesterday. He's getting a 10-day furlough starting this week and after that he's going overseas, sometime in June. Yes, he's really going this time. He didn't seem too worried. Guess he realizes there's not much he can do about it. He said he'll keep in touch with me.

Haven't heard from Rum for 3 weeks now. Wonder if he went to New York this past weekend? And if he did, whether he looked up the Rose girl – I gave him her address.

We're still very busy at the office, even with the extra help. The sergeant who is to take my place is working tonight.

Received a wedding announcement from Dziuvau's, stating that Dorothy has been married.

Well, I arrived here six months ago today. Also on a Monday. Seems I've lived here longer than that, because I know so many people here. Beth and I get invitations to dinner from different people, all the time.

Well, so long for now.

Love & Kisses

Ed

HEADQUARTERS
REPLACEMENT AND SCHOOL COMMAND

Army Ground Forces
Birmingham, Alabama
Sunday Afternoon
12:15 o'clock
28 May 1944

Dear Mother –

Stopped in here for just a few minutes to see whether there was any mail for me. Your Thursday evening letter was here and a couple editions of the Buflo News. Last Friday morning I received your letter which said that you had sent my watch out that day. On Friday afternoon the watch arrived here in the same length of time as the letter. Thanks a lot, it's nice to have it back again. It arrived safely, but of course, it would have as you had packed it so well.

You mentioned that it would be nice if I could be reassigned to Washington, D.C. I suppose it would, but if I could be sent there then I could also stay here. As it is now I'll be assigned to some regiment or division. Of course, I'll be doing the same type of work as I am now, in some headquarters. I'm going to ask for my furlough in about 10 days or so I guess. Just waiting to see if I can find out my next assignment.

So Donnie had his hair cut. I'll bet he does look different. It'll be cooler for him anyway & he'll look like a boy. It's really hot here today; about 90° now I guess.

That was very nice of you to send a birthday card to Estelle's nephew. I can imagine that the boys overseas appreciate anything like that.

Last night Beth and I went to some people we know in Homewood. Homewood is the same to B'ham as Kenmore is to Buffalo. Very nice residential section. There we had supper out in their large backyard. We fried hamburgers and hot dogs over an open fire. It really tasted good. They have a combination radio and phonograph player which cost $750.00. Also have about $50 worth of records. Very good ones too. We played "William Tell Overture" some of Chopins' waltzes played by Paderewski and others.

Tell Adeline that I've received her letter and will write to her one of these days. Right now I'll have to go home for dinner. So long and hope I'll see you in about 3 weeks.

Love & Kisses

Ed

Friday

11:30 PM

2 June 44

Dear Mother –

Just a few words before going to bed. Beth and I went to the movies tonight right after work. Saw "Cover Girl" a very good musical in Technicolor.

Received your Tuesday eve letter today. Had a letter from Rum a couple of days ago. He said he was planning on going to New York City this weekend.

No, I haven't heard from Bob. I sent him a short note when I was home on furlough, but never received an answer.

Also this week received a letter from Norman Blue. He's one of the fellows with whom I worked in Massena and N. Y. and who went to Africa. He's still there and has seen quite a few places like Jerusalem, Bethlehem, Nazareth, etc. He said that is now Colonel Sibley, who is stationed in England.

Well, it's going to happen again! Two soldiers are going to take my place when I leave. The same thing happened when I quit Down's and International Milling. It seems I always do work of two people. Of course, I've been more appreciated in the Army as I have the highest rank possible as a non-commissioned officer.

Haven't heard anything further as yet about my transfer.

Am enclosing $150.00 in money order. You can't get more than $100.00 on one money order, so that's why I'm sending two.

Received a letter from Ronnie today. He told me mostly about what he did while home on furlough. He likes Butch, Donnie & Sharon.

Well, tomorrow's Saturday and I have the afternoon off. Beth's parents, and she and I may go out to their cabin and spend the weekend there. It would be fun.

Well, the invasion hasn't started as yet and I was sure it could be in May.

So long for now and I'm still hoping to be home this month. Goodnight.

Love & Kisses

Ed

Hotel Piccadilly
227 West 45th Street
At Broadway
New York

Saturday

Dear Mother –

In New York this weekend as you can see. Came in last night and staying till tomorrow.

It's cool here compared to Washington. New York is still New York. Exciting and crowded as ever before.

Went down to the Engineers on Wall St. and on Broadway. Most everyone is in the Army or Navy all over the World.

Saw Ed's girlfriend, later went to her hotel but she had a previous date so I left early. It's only 9:00 P. M. now so I will go out and see what's cooking.

Received socks and cigarets you sent. Thank you very much.

There's nothing new in Washington. Expect to be home in 2 weeks for Saturday and all day Sunday unless my plans are changed.

Love

Rum

M/Sgt. Edward F. Bartz
Co. "E" Bks. 119
Cp. Ritchie, Md.

Sunday
9:15 AM
25 June 44

Dear Mother:

Arrived here at 2:15 yesterday afternoon. Took a bus from Hagerstown, Md., instead of waiting for the train. The camp is way up, about 2,000 feet above sea level and the air is good.

I don't know as yet what I'm going to do and if I did I'm not allowed to tell anyone. I'm to be interviewed tomorrow. Don't know <u>what</u> I'll do, how long I'll be here or whether I <u>will</u> stay here.

We have to get up at 5:15 AM which is the earliest I've had in any camp. Breakfast is at 5:30. We have no sheets here, but sleep right under the blankets.

There's only one mass at the Chapel here on Sunday and that's at 6:40 AM. Went this morning.

Sure was glad you gave me that fruit. It was good and I ate all of it. Have the candy here with me in the barracks.

It's quite cool here and I've been wearing my jacket. It's a good thing I brought my overalls. That's all we wear here.

Can't tell you very much about the post, except that it's quite small and quite nice.

I can't leave the post for 7 days, as that's a regulation for new men coming in.

So long for now. My address is
    Co ."E" Bks. 119
    Camp Ritchie, Md.
<u>Do not</u> put MITC. So long. I'll try to call today.

Love & Kisses

Ed

Roman holding Sharon O'Hara and Edward holding Butch O'Hara.

Postcard –

Thursday

8:25 AM

27 July 44

Just coming into St. Paul, Minn., and will try to mail this there.
Had a swell time in Chicago. More later.

Love

Ed

Postcard –

Thursday

3:35 P. M.

27 July 44

Hello there –

    Am writing this on the train and will mail from Aberdeen, S. Dakota. Peggy's father got a berth for me. Feeling fine. Will arrive Wash Sat noon.

               Love
               Ed

Postcard –

Friday
9:55 AM
MNT
28 July 44

    Going thru beautiful country. Writing this on the train. Mountains all around us. 24 more hours to go. Have now travelled 2,000 miles.

Love

Ed

M/Sgt. Edward F. Bartz
Co. "D" 160th Med. Tng. Bn.
ASFTC
Ft. Lewis, Washington

Saturday
7:05 PM PWT
5 August 1944

Dear Mother:

Yesterday I received your letter of last Friday. Of course, some of the time in getting here was caused because I've been transferred from one battalion to another. Now that I'll be in this company for about 3 months it should come in much faster.

Well, here I am in Charge of Quarters again. You will remember that last Saturday I was doing the same job. So that spoils another weekend for me. Of course, with my rank I have to expect responsibility and work while the privates and others go to town and have a good time.

We start training next Monday and that should continue for about 14 weeks. Then, as I guess I told you before, I'll be assigned to some hospital either in this country or overseas. I'll be getting a good assignment out of it too, either as a Chief Clerk or a Sergeant Major. That'll be about the middle of November and who knows how the war will be going then.

This new company I'm in is way out in the woods. There are a lot of evergreen trees around and the air is good, even though we are only about 60 feet above sea level. Buffalo is about 600 feet above sea level, so you can see how low we are. This will give you an idea how far out in the woods we are. This afternoon three deer came out of the woods and walked around near our barracks, then became frightened and ran away. The other day a young four point buck came right up to our mess hall and wasn't frightened at all, and let us pet him. Guess he was hungry.

I'm glad you went to see "Going My Way." I saw the picture "Liberation of Rome" at Camp Ritchie, a week after it had been taken. It was restricted at the time.

It seems strange for me, a Master Sergeant, to be taking basic training, but I felt better after I found that there's another M/Sgt who's in this company, and also two First Sgts. One of them has been in the army for 6 years. Also there's a sergeant who was with the Infantry in Italy and was wounded there; had shrapnel in the legs. He's going to take the training too.

I've been getting quite a few letters from Beth. She started writing the day I left Birmingham and has written one every day.

It's quite cool here, at least it seems that way to me. During the day I wear my coveralls with a sweat shirt underneath. In the evening I wear my woolen uniform, which I had with me. My laundry from Ritchie hasn't arrived as yet, and we haven't sent out any from here, until next Monday, so I've been washing out my underwear, sox and handkerchiefs. That, together with basic training makes me feel as if I just come into army, if it wasn't for six stripes on my sleeve.

I'm going to be on duty here in the office until 12 noon tomorrow, with time off to go to church. Then I guess I'll go in to Tacoma, a city of about 100,000 population, 17 miles from here. One of the fellows I knew at Ritchie, lives in this vicinity and knows some people in Tacoma, so he gave me a letter of introduction to them, so that will help some in making some friends there.

I saw a car here on the post with Buffalo license plates on it. Guess it belongs to some officer. It sure seemed strange to see Buffalo plates way over here.

Well, I'll say goodnight for now.

Love and Kisses,

Ed

Wednesday
1:00 pm
9 Aug 44

Dear Mother –
    This is my lunch hour, but I just wanted to drop you a line to let you know that my address has again been changed, but I'm still in the same barracks:
        Co. "F" PROVISIONAL REGIMENT
        M. T. S. – ASFTC

You can abbreviate as follows:
        Co. "F" Prov. Regt.
        M.T.S. – ASFTC

        S'long.

        Love

        Ed

Co. "B" 162nd M.T.B.
MTS – ASFTC

Sunday
2:30 PM
13. Aug. '44

Dear Mother –
Received your packages with the caps, ties and handkerchief. Thanks a lot.

I haven't heard from you for quite some time now. In past I haven't had a single letter from you addressed to me since I sent you my address from the 154th Bn. I did get two of them from you addressed to "ASFTC – (MD).

Of course, you may have written but since I've been moving around so much I guess the mail hasn't kept up with me. You know now that I have a new address, as I sent you a postcard to that effect. The strange part is that I had my address changed to the present one, without moving an inch. You see they organized this new regiment and automatically assigned us to it.

Well, I finished my first week of school yesterday; seven more to go. Once a week we have regular field training such as marching, exercises, playing ball, etc. Yesterday was our day. It felt good to be outdoors from 8 AM until 5:30 PM. Oh yes, we went to see an Army movie called "Battle of Russia", which I had seen at R&SC in Birmingham, but which is very interesting.

I guess one of these weekends I'll take a trip to Mt. Rainier. Didn't feel like going anywhere today.

I haven't as yet been paid; not since June 30; so I'll get two month's pay on August 31st. I have about eight dollars now, which might not be enough to last for more than two weeks. Could you send me about $15.00, please. I might want to go somewhere for a weekend.

I suppose you know that Pres. Roosevelt spoke from the Puget Sound Navy Yard last night. That's about 50 miles from here.

The weather has warmed up a bit today, but it's cloudy almost every day.

Will you please also send me the book in the chifferobe called "The Robe". I've been doing some reading here from books in the library. Now that I have the time I'll read that book. First of all please take out the pressed gardenia which is in the book, and save it for me somewhere. It's the one Beth wore on our last date in June. Just wrap the book well and tell them at the Post office that it's a book. They send books at the rate of 64 per pound.

Well, so long for now and hope I'll hear from you soon.

Love & Kisses
Ed

Tuesday
8:30 PM
15 Aug. '44

Dear Mother –

Yesterday, I believe, I wrote you saying I wasn't getting any mail from you. Now it's starting to come in. Of course, the letters first go to the 154th, then to the 160th and finally here. I received one from you yesterday and another one today.

Also a letter from Rum. The reason he moved I guess is 'cause his room was so small, only a little bigger than your bathroom and didn't have a regular bed in it, only sort of a couch. Now he has a larger room.

I now stay in a "private" room. There are three other soldiers here with me: M/Sgt. Steward, about 35 years old, English ancestry, comes from Kansas and worked for the government before he came into the Army. He's married.

Then there's Tech. Sgt. O'Regan, Irish naturally. He's a Catholic and we go to church together. He's 37 years old, an accountant and comes from New York City. He's married too.

Then there's Staff Sgt. Louis Rubenfeld, 28 years old, a Jew, lawyer, from Peekskill, N.Y. Single.

The four of us get along together very well.

It seems strange to read about the heat in Chicago, Buffalo and New York City. Here it's very cool all the time and I wear my woolen uniform at night and also a jacket. I wear a sweat shirt in bed.

Yes, I have Irene's address and have written to her.

Tomorrow is our field day, which we get once a week, and we're having a 10-mile hike.

Went to church at noon today with O'Regan. They also had a mass tonite in case someone could not make it during the day.

I'll say goodnight for now.

Love,

Ed

P. S. You don't have to use that address which I have on the back of the envelope. I just put it there for the fun of it.

Master Sergeant Edward Francis Joseph Bartz, 32212187
Company "B" Barracks 603-A Second Floor
162nd Medical Training Battaliion – 40th Medical Training Regiment
Medical Training Section – Army Service Forces Training Ctr.
Fort Lewis, Pierce County, Washington
United States of America
West Hemisphere

Tuesday Evening
7:00 O'Clock
22 August 1944
Pacific War Time

Dear Mother:

We're quite busy at school this week. Tonight, Thursday night and Friday night we are having classes in addition to the day classes. Right now we have some free time so I thought I'd send you a letter. This is the only kind of paper I have with me so I'll use it as stationery.

I suppose you have my card from Olympia by now. It's a nice, little city. A lot of trees and flowers all around, which make it seem quiet and peaceful. The population is only about 14,000 people. It's the capital of the state of Washington. I went through the capitol building and it's very beautiful inside, as well as on the outside. One of the main industries of Olympia is oysters, for which it is quite famous. It's located right on Puget Sound. The town is only 16 miles from camp, the same as Tacoma only in the opposite direction. The round trip via bus is 35 cents. Not many soldiers go there as there isn't much to do, but I like to go there and just visit. It's a pleasure in itself not to have to look at a lot of uniforms.

The money order arrived yesterday morning, which was very quick as you sent it out on Saturday morning; only 2 days. Thanks a lot. It came just in time as I was down to my last penny.

Here's something that may seem strange to you, but it's true nevertheless: I'm about as near to Russia as I am to Buffalo. It's approximately 2,400 airline miles from Ft. Lewis to Siberia and about the same to Buffalo, maybe a little less. Astounding, isn't it. You can look at an airmap and see for yourself.

I joined the Sergeant's Club here at Ft. Lewis for one month. It's a nice place to go for a glass of beer or something to eat. Also they have dances. Only Sergeants are allowed and have to show their membership card before they can go in. The dues are 75 cents per month.

Well, I'll say goodnight for now. Thanks again for the money order.

Love and kisses

Ed

August 23, 1944
Washington, D.C.

Dear Mother –

Received your letter a couple days ago and also the package the other day. You sent me plenty of shirts but I can use them all. I'm wearing one right now and it's a pleasure to change from the whites in the evening.

My trip back to Washington wasn't bad coming from Buffalo because I was in an air-conditioned car and it was quite clean. Got into D.C. about 10:00 A.M., and at work by eleven o'clock. It's been cool around here lately but raining now and then. The apartment is coming along quite well and I like it much better then a single room any time.

Guess I'll stay in D. C. this weekend as I don't especially care to go any place. A girl I use to know in Canada has just returned from Fairbanks, Alaska and lives in Baltimore. I might go down next week and see her.

Has Freeman returned yet? I suppose he has as he didn't expect to stay very long.

Received a letter from Ed several days ago. He has a new address again.

It won't be long now before the war will be over at least in Europe and maybe it won't take as long as we expect to defeat the Japanese.

Thanks for sending the sheets, trousers, shirts and Camels. There isn't any store around here and I have been out of cigarets several times so the carton comes in handy. Been having a little work at the office lately so haven't had a chance to write from there. In the evening there is generally someone over the apartment, so that doesn't give me much time

Yes, I've been getting your letters regularly now and one from Mamie. I received a letter from Sgt. Di Pasquale the other day. He's with the infantry somewhere in England (or did I tell you this before?)

After we finish school at the end of September we might have a couple of weeks of bivouac. That means marching away from camp, etc., and sleeping on the ground at night. So I guess I'd better get ready to keep warm. Will you please send me my army winter underwear. I have it in a box, somewhere in the closet I guess. Also I could use about 3 additional suits of summer underwear.

It's been rather warm during the day lately. Went up to 80° one day. Of course, to you that would seem cool after all the heat you've had in Buflo. either. In fact we just got rid of about 5 people and its only 11:00 P. M. so I decided to write.

That's all for now.

Love
Rum

Friday Evening
9:00 o'clock
25 August '44

Dear Mother –

Received your Sunday evening letter this afternoon. "The Robe" arrived this morning. Thanks.

Well, here I am still school tonight; we are having class until 10 o'clock and I happen to have a little free time now. I sure have been kept busy.

They sure are strict at this camp. Particularly here at the school. For instance, we have to get a haircut every week; shine shoes every day; clean fingernails every day; shave every day. And on Friday instead of mapping the wooden floors like I've done in other camps, we have to scrub with brush and soap and hot water, until the floor is almost white. Of course, I realize that it's all for our own good.

I was planning to go to Mt. Rainier this coming Sunday but I have to go on duty as Charge of Quarters on Sunday afternoon at 5:30 to be on duty all night, so I can't go very far this coming weekend. That will be the third weekend during which I had to work. That's what I get for having such a high rank. Some of the lieutenants say they've been here for three months and haven't had a Sunday off. Don't know if it's true or not.

Speaking about being strict: One fellow here at Lewis ran away for a month and they found him somewhere in Oregon a couple of weeks ago. He was tried by a court martial and dishonorable discharged from the Army and sentenced to 5 years at hard labor at the Federal Penitentiary at Fort Leavenworth. They don't fool around over here. I guess they read that order to us as sort of a warning.

Have you heard from Freeman as yet, or do you have any idea where he is? Seems strange that he just walked out like that. Thanks for the clippings from the News about the flood and also about George's barn burning down. That sure was too bad.

It's raining tonight and the first rain we've had since I've been here, I believe. It's not raining hard, just a drizzle.

Yes, I've been receiving your letters alright now. You asked whether I've been coming in alright now that I'm settled in one place, but before they too were late in coming. Yesterday I received a copy of the Buflo Eve News dated July 20th. It had been forwarded from Ritchie over a month ago.

As I said we're really busy. We got off from school this afternoon at 3:30 instead of 5:20 as usual, but I was busy every minute until 8:00 o'clock when I had to come to school again tonight. I helped scrub the floor and then had to get all my clothes ready for tomorrows inspection.

Incidentally, here's something I'd appreciate as a birthday gift. About four pair of white shorts, that is if you can get white. I guess I asked you for some suits of summer underwear in my previous letter, but I just noticed tonight when I was getting my foot locker in order, that I have quite a few undershirts but not quite enough shorts; only about seven pair counting what I have in the laundry. I think you'd better get size 36 instead of 34, too.

Now that I have "The Robe" I don't know when I'll get a chance to read it, what with all my various tasks to do. Incidentally, I've finished another subject at school. This time I received a "Superior" on my final exam. That's anywhere from 96 to 100%. The other mark I had was "Excellent". That's about 90 to 95%.

I hope to have some extra time so that I can again visit the people whom I met at Interlaaken, Tacoma.

I guess I've told you about the Irish fellow who sleeps in the same room as I do. He's from New York City, and his name is O'Regan. Well, this morning I was talking to him and I guess we happened to be speaking about foreign languages and he mentioned that his wife was Polish. I happened to think that it's like Adeline and Milton. He's 37 years old and a Catholic. Really has an Irish brogue too.

Well, I'll say so long for now. Good night.

Love

Ed

Wednesday afternoon
1:05 o'clock, 6 September '44

Dear Mother –

Just a few words this afternoon. The package with the underwear, after shave lotion, etc., arrived at noon today. Thanks a lot. While at Benning I loaned it to a fellow who needed one and didn't have any at the time; then he was transferred and forgot to return it. It'll have to eventually come out of my pay; only about 75 cents I guess. It sure has been hot lately. Yesterday it reached 92° and that seemed hot, after all the cold weather we've been having. I read in last nite's paper about the earthquake back East and down South. I notice that Malone, N. Y., got the most of it. That's 37 miles east of Massena. Did you feel any of it?

Beth has two weeks vacation, which started last Monday. She's spending this week in Atlanta with her aunt. Next week she'll be home she said just to take things easy and get some things done around the house, also. I'm going to visit those people whom I met a few weeks ago. Am going this Sunday afternoon. I guess I told Adeline about this.

Your letter of last Thursday arrived yesterday. Thanks a lot for the dollar. I had to borrow a couple of dollars last Sunday from one of the fellows in my room. We signed the pay roll a couple of days ago, which means that we'll be paid either this Saturday or next Monday. I've got two month's pay coming. The lieutenant told us that we might get a furlough after finishing school and training. I guess we'll get paid the first of the month again, so I can retain money for train fare just in case we do get a furlough. The coach fare from here to Buffalo is about $65.00; Pullman is about $100.00.

The war news sure does look good. The European war might still end around my birthday. I guess you know about my trip to Seattle and the boat trip, from my letter to Adeline. I visited an acquarium in Seattle which had all the fish that are found in Puget Sound in Seattle. There sure is a variety, including an octopus which they had.

Well, I'll say so long for now until the next time.

Love,
Ed

THURSDAY MORNING
10:00
7 Sept. '44

DEAR MOTHER:
    JUST WANT TO DROP A NOTE AND MAIL AT NOON.
WILL YOU PLEASE SEND ME MY CAMERA AND ANY 616
FILM WHICH MIGHT BE THERE. SEND IT INSURED PARCEL
POST.
    WE'RE ALLOWED TO HAVE CAMERAS WITH US AND
I'M SORRY I DID NOT HAVE IT WITH ME AT MT. RAINIER,
SEATTLE AND OTHER PLACES. HOWEVER, I'LL STILL BE
ABLE TO GET SOMETHING INTERESTING PICTURES, I
GUESS.
    SO LONG FOR NOW.

                LOVE,
                Ed

Monday morning
11:05 o'clock
11 Sept. '44

Dear Mother –

Well, here I go starting the sixth week of school, with two more to follow.

Yesterday, at 1:30 PM, I went to visit the Strong family in Tacoma. They met me after I got off the bus, and let me drive the car back to the house. Incidentally, they have three cars in the family. It was a warm day so we went in swimming right in the lake, which is actually in their back yard, if you want to call it that. The water is cold all the time, as the lake is fed by mountain streams.

Later, at about 4 o'clock, we had some tea and sandwiches on the terrace. It was a congenial gathering. Later went into the house and I played their phonograph player. They sure have a good selection of records too.

Two of the girls will be going to college this month: Jeane, who is 17, will go to Stanford in California as a freshman and "Bibbits" (Elizabeth) 20 years of age, will go to the University of Oregon in Oregon, as a junior. They're both very attractive girls.

They sure have a lot of fruit trees on their grounds, such as cherry, prune, plum, pear. The cherries are still on the trees. In fact the whole state of Washington seems to have a lot of fruit trees and berry bushes. We have a lot of them right in camp. The soil is supposed to be so fertile from the former volcanoes which used to exist many years ago around here.

I'm glad to hear that "Butch's" illness was only a sore throat and nothing worse. I've received letters from Adeline and you, something last week; I think they were written on Sept. 4th. They're back at the barracks, so I'm not sure.

I think we should get paid today; I hope so anyway.

I guess I didn't finish telling about my visit to the Strong's yesterday. They had some more company come in about 7:00 PM, who left about 2 hours later. Then we had dinner, which was very good, topped off with fresh peach shortcake & cream. I left there at 11:30 PM and they drove me to the place where I could catch a bus back to camp. So I had quite an enjoyable day. They asked me to come again.

Well, I'll say so long for now. Class will soon be over, or I should say this open hour, will be. Then we'll go back to the barracks for dinner.

Love,
Ed

Saturday Morning
8:35 o'clock
16 September '44

Dear Mother:

We had inspection this morning and came to school a little while ago and have a little spare time before classes begin. It sure is cold today.

Well, we got paid yesterday but they made a mistake on my payroll. Instead of getting $240.58 which was due me, after all deductions were made, I received only $95.68, which is less than one month's pay and I was supposed to get two month's. So I told the lieutenant about it and they're checking. There's another M/Sgt. who's short exactly the same amount as I am, that is $144.90.

Here's what I'm going to do as soon as I get a little time. Take out a Class E Allotment, which means that they'll deduct the money from my pay and send you a check.

Even though I don't get paid for two months, like I haven't been for the past two, you'll still get the money. That way you'll get the money and if I need it I can write to you. I'll have about $75 deducted. You'll notice that the bonds have been coming in to you, yet I haven't been paid; that the same way that'll work.

There's also another allotment which has been in operation since July 1942, I believe. It's the Class F allotment. If you were more than 50% dependent upon me then I could have $22 per month deducted from my pay and the government would add $28 to it, making $50 per month you'd get. If you're less that 50% dependent on me, they'd take $22 from my pay and add only $15, giving you $37 per month. I was thinking about taking that out too.

Some forms would have to be filled out, however, and statements made by two of your neighbors that you're dependent on me. In the case of a wife, it's automatic however, in fact they'll deduct it from a husband if he likes it or not, as long as the wife lets the army know about it.

I won't send any money home now until I find out about the $144.90 additional I'm supposed to get. You can't tell I might get a furlough next month and we're not getting paid the first of October, like we're supposed to. It seems they've got everything mixed up here. I've never seen anything like it.

I'll say so long for now.

Love,
Ed

PS: Nine years ago today, Adeline and I started school at Chown's and here I am still going to school.

E.

Incidentally, a couple of weeks ago I wrote in to Albany, N. Y., requesting a war ballot and it arrived yesterday. So now I can vote for President any time I want to, as long as the ballot reaches Albany by November 3rd. All I have to do is mark it the way I want to and mail it back. Guess, I'll vote for Roosevelt again.

Ed

19 Sept. 1944

Dear Mother –

Received your letter today and also one from Mamie. The cake came yesterday and is very good. Also received the blue uniforms with cigarets. Thank you for sending everything.

We put on our blue uniforms on the 1st of October. It has been quite warm here lately but not hot. It is very damp however and we have been getting plenty of rain.

Spent the weekend before in New York. Stayed in D. C. last time and expect to stay here this coming weekend.

Played some football tonight. Have bowling on Wednesday nights.

Still expect to be home around the 11th of October which is about 3 weeks from now, and the way time has been passing it won't be long. I'll be glad to get away from here for awhile.

Haven't heard from Ed lately. Maybe I owe him a letter.

Also received a letter from Adeline yesterday. She told me about the accident Sharon Ann had, Mamie did also. Hope she wasn't hurt too badly.

Understand the O'Hara's expect to move sometimes in October. Maybe I'm coming home at the wrong time.

The apartment looks pretty good now. Even have a rug and drapes now.

Not much more to say.

Love

Rum

Wednesday Afternoon
1:05 o'clock
20 September '44

Dear Mother:

Received your Thursday letter today. The camera arrived yesterday, but I wasn't able to pick it up until this morning. In your previous letter you mentioned that you weren't sure whether you had sent my camera or Rums. Last night I happened to be at the Post Exchange Store and found out that they had just received a shipment of films. Only one roll was allowed to a customer and I didn't know what size to get, as the camera which you sent is mine. Incidentally, that film which you also sent was some which I got in Birmingham, but does not fit my camera so I sold it to a fellow here who has that size camera. They don't get film very often here on the post but when they do it goes in a hurry.

You'll probably be soon getting the record which I made on my birthday. Let me know just what Butch says when he hears me talking to him on the record.

I'm glad to hear that Sharon is feeling better. Have you thought anything about getting your eyes examined for a pair of glasses?

Last night I had to get some shots such as Typhoid and smallpox. You see, you will have to get them every so often. They're really not overseas shots as yet. Those would probably be yellow fever, malaria, etc., depending where the person is going.

Well, I've had my uniform cleaned and pressed for the graduation exercises which will be held a week from this Saturday afternoon. The general will be there and I believe he's the one who gives out the diplomas.

The weather has been rather cloudy lately. We had an earthquake at 1:20 yesterday morning, but I slept right through it. It was supposed to have rattled things around a bit.

Well, so long for now. Incidentally, I received a letter from Mamie yesterday, and I had just sent one to her a few hours before that. She asked about a certain negative, of Rum and I, together with Dutchess. Any negatives taken recently should be in one of those small drawers in the dresser, unless Rum took some when he was home last.

Love,
Ed

PS: I've taken out the Class E Allotment and they'll start deducting $75.00 each month from my pay and send you the check. The first one probably won't come until about the middle of October, as it takes some time to get the whole thing started. They haven't as yet given me the rest of the money, which is due me, $144.90, but they're working on it. Some clerk made a mistake in making the payroll.

Tuesday Afternoon
1:11 o'clock
26 Sept. '44

Dear Mother:

Just a few words as I wrote to you yesterday afternoon. I received a letter from Rum yesterday and he said that he didn't know whether it was his turn or mine to write. This was last Friday. The strange part is that I wrote him a letter just about the same time and said the same thing. So our letters passed each going across the country.

He mentioned about going home next month. I guess I won't be able to be home then, but maybe he can come in for the weekend, IF I do get furlough after all my training.

Incidentally, I tried to transfer to the Infantry at Benning but the regulations here state that we can't do it. But maybe I'll get so that I like it in the Medical Department, you can't tell. The advantage of being with the division at Benning is that I'd be with officers who really know me. Also having been in the Infantry I seem to prefer it.

I lost the spring-bars on my wrist watch and tried to get some here but had no luck. I wrote Beth about it and she was able to get me a couple in Birmingham, and sent them to me.

Rum mentioned that he was in New York City several weeks ago and also in Baltimore to stay for the weekend.

The weather has been quite pleasant lately. I only hope that it keeps up during the time we're training out in the field.

Well, so long for this time.

Love,
Ed

PS: Will you please put the enclosed envelop in my scrapbook. Thanks.

E.

2 October 1944
Washington, D. C.

Dear Mother –

Received your letter last week. Might have been mixed up with the one you said you didn't send.

Put on our blue uniforms yesterday, and since it has been cool lately they are comfortable enough.

Haven't gone anyplace now in 3 weeks. Next weekend is the one I have off but I intend to stay here again.

Still expect to come a week from Wednesday.

Have been doing the same old stuff around here.

Received a letter from Ed last week. Says he is almost finished with his training.

How are things at home? Are the O'Hara's getting ready to move?

Been having dinner at different places, being invited out about every 3rd night.

Get paid tomorrow which is a good thing.

Hardly anything to say. When in New York saw the movie "Arsenic and Old Lace." It's very good. If the picture is in town you should go down and see it.

How does Freeman feel lately?

Wondering if that 3 tons of coal will arrive when I'm home. I don't know if I would be up to it now. Just don't do those things now days.

About all for now –

Love

Rum

30 October 1944

Dear Mother –

It's almost a week since I returned to Washington and most everything remained the same except that the civilian supervisor is on vacation which makes it fine for everyone because no one likes him but who does like supervisors?

The train was fairly full of passengers until we got into Pennsylvania and then the train started to become crowded, especially when the last car was taken off and everyone had to find seats who had been in that car.

Wednesday was bowling nite but I didn't do so good because I was out of practice.

Thursday I went to the Hotel Statler to a dance that the office held. That was some night but I took in the beauty of the hotel and glamour of the ballroom early in the evening, enough to appreciate it. Didn't get to bed till 4 and had to get up a little after 7. The war was held up next day as far as I was concerned.

Had a letter waiting for me from Daniel upon my return. He is still now in Belgium, and says that he is living in a hotel, far better than it was France. He got a chance to visit Paris while in France.

Friday I went to bed quite early, that is laid down on the couch and fell asleep. Woke up about 11 and then went to bed but couldn't fall asleep till 3, so I'll never do that again.

Saturday night I had a date till 12:00 then came home. At 1 I went out again to meet the girl I've been going around with as she works on the night shift. Well I'm glad it was Sunday next day.

Sunday a couple of Waves brought over a chicken and we had fried chicken but they must have done something wrong because it didn't taste like your chickens.

Tonight is Monday, almost Tuesday now, but I washed out my socks which I should say was about 20 pair because they are strung clear across a 20 foot clothes line. My roommate is in bed, but I don't feel sleepy so I figured I'd write this letter.

Received your package today. It was so heavy that I thought you sent a china set because the label said "Handle with Care – Glass". But it was the fruit that made it so.

Enclosed is an article from our weekly newspaper put out in the office.

Outside of this rambling there is no more so thank you for the fruit and candy and the trouble in sending the package. I'll write again.

Love
Rum

14 November 1944

Dear Mother –

Received your letter about a week ago. So here goes another one back to you.

Saw the Navy-Notre Dame football game over in Baltimore a week ago. It was a very good game since Navy won. There was a crown of over 65,000 people in the stadium. The city was certainly jammed too, all the restaurants, bars and such were full. A fellow I work with has a car and he drove us down. He took his wife and I had a Wave with me. We stopped at a barndance out in the country on the way back. That certainly was a sight.

This coming Saturday is my day off but I'm staying in town. I'm going down to the Navy Yard and try to get a coat for Milton. He likes them and they are quite a bargain.

The weather has been pretty nice around here. It's been warm and haven't had any rain in sometime.

Incidentally I had my pajamas hanging out on the line Halloween Night and some kids swiped the tops from one pair and the bottom from the other. Consequently I have only one pair now and it doesn't match. So if you please, would you send a couple of pairs that I might have around the house.

They are already planning for a Christmas party and its still over a month away. I don't believe I'll even try to get home for Christmas, the time would be too short and the trains too crowded.

Please don't get anything for me. And tell Adeline and Mamie not too either because I won't get a chance to do any shopping so I think that just sending a card will have to do this year. Besides there isn't anything worthwhile buying.

With this thought, I leave and say goodnight –

Love
Rum

Sunday Afternoon
24 December 1944
3:10 o'clock

Dear Mother:

Well, here it is the day before Christmas, but of course we won't have any snow up here, although it is very cold. The temperature today is about 30 degrees.

Yesterday afternoon we went for a 7-mile hike, wearing full field packs, gas masks and water canteens. It was a perfect day, sun shining and the temperature about 29 degrees. Really felt good after it was over.

There's still nothing about our transfer but it'll no doubt come after Christmas. Probably I'll be spending New Year's Eve on the train. I know definitely that I'll be transferred to another camp, but don't know where as yet. I've just been reading about 80,000 men to be transferred from the Air Corps and also the Army Service Forces, (which I'm in now) into the Infantry as they are now short of men.

Received your card with $5 yesterday. Thanks a lot.

I'm going to Midnight Mass tonight and will receive Holy Communion. Also received Communion this morning at Mass. The chapel was nicely decorated with poinsettias, etc.

I'm enclosing Milton's car registration license, which I forgot to return upon leaving last Sunday. Have they moved as yet?

Well, I guess that's about all for now. So long and Merry Christmas to you.

Love –
Ed

4 January 1945

Dear Mother –

You are probably wondering what has happened to me. The time has passed so quickly that I didn't have a chance to really write a letter.

I received your Christmas presents of fruitcake, cigarettes and candy. Still have the fruitcake. Also received a carton of cigarettes from Mamie and a pair of pajamas.

Had plenty to do around here at Christmas time. Was invited to 3 different places for dinner. Spent the afternoon of Christmas at one girl's place and the evening at 2 others. Called you up about 11:30 Christmas Night. The call went thru in less than a minute but you weren't home.

New Year's Eve I had a little gathering in the afternoon and in the evening we went to another party so I spent quite a busy New Year's Eve. Had to work New Years Day too. We got off for Christmas however. Also had a party in the office the Saturday before Christmas. Really had a time.

One of the fellows from the office went on leave for 2 weeks and he gave me his car to use which came in quite handy.

Understand that you have quite of bit of snow in Buffalo. Just had a couple of snowflakes around here and there isn't any on the ground at all. It's very warm today too. Got a card from Daniel in Paris. Also one from Whitehouse, Yukon.

Glad that you bought a coat for yourself.

Don't know Adeline's new address. Just know that its on Highgate.

Had a card from Ed for Christmas which was sent from Buffalo. Haven't heard from him since however.

Still doing the same work. Might get a chance to go to Pearl Harbor. They need about 6 or 7 of us out there and there's only 15 of us here.

Thank you for the Christmas presents and also Christmas and New Year's card and also for the five dollars.

That's all for now –

Love
Rum
Co. "B" 57th I.T.B.
Camp Howze, Texas

Sunday Afternoon
4:20 PM
14 January 1945

Dear Mother –

We sure have been busy during the past week and I haven't been able to write any letters. It seems that Sunday will be my only day for correspondence.

We train out in the field all day and then at night we non-commissioned officers have to go to school. Also scrub the barracks, clean rifles, equipment, etc. I've been going to bed near midnight.

Incidentally, this camp comes under Replacement and School Command and they do the assigning. It seems strange, last year I was in the Hq and now here I am taking training.

I'm really getting toughened up in this training. My cold is all gone. Tomorrow at 4 AM we are going to march to the rifle range.

We were interviewed and I found out why I didn't stay at Camp Ritchie in the Military Intelligence. While there they took an x-ray of my injured knee, and I noticed on my record (although I wasn't supposed to) that there's a notation on it: "NOT TO HAVE LONG MARCHES, STANDING OR JUMPING." That seems ironic, doesn't it? I've been doing all that, even when my knee hurt me. So they disqualified me from MITC and here I am in the Infantry.

I've written to Major Ash, who now more or less can help to assign me, about transferring to that division at Benning, but he wrote and said it couldn't be done now, as I'm a trainee. I'm really getting tired of training.

I've received all your letters sent to Lewis, including the one you sent here addressed "157th M.T.B."

I'm glad you like your new coat. I received a letter from Rum and he seemed to have quite a good holiday season. Also mentioned that he might go to Pearl Harbor.

Received a card from Al, with $2.00. I'll have to write him & thank him for that.

I want to close this letter soon and get away from the barracks for awhile.

So long and I'll try to write before next Sunday.

Love –

Ed

Tuesday
8:00 PM
16 January '45

Dear Mother –

I have a few spare moments before we have to go to a meeting, so I'll write only a few words. We keep on the go like this all day, and when we're finished I'm ready to go to bed.

Would you please send me a half-dozen pair of some kind of woolen socks. We march about 10 miles per day and they're better than cotton. Also I'm having trouble in keeping my feet warm in the cold mornings and nights.

They have no socks on the whole post either for issue or sale.

Also will you please send me some candy. They don't have any on this post, in fact they have nothing. At other camps I could buy candy bars, etc., and I miss not having any candy. Make it some mixed chocolates and also some fudge. Incidentally Beth made some fudge for me for Xmas and sent it to Lewis. It arrived here a few days ago, a little white, after more than 5,000 miles of travel, but still good.

In regard to the socks which I want: they don't have to be all wool. Also the color doesn't matter, but white or gray would be best. I'll wear them with my high shoes and leggings so they're not seen. Of course, they'll have to be long socks, and not ankle ones. Doesn't Free wear socks like those for work?

Yes, we sure keep busy. We leave here when it's dark and come back when it's dark. However, I really am feeling good and feel as if I could lick a wildcat barehanded, almost! I'm eating like a horse, but keeping slim. The exercises we get are really toughening. Of course, I would like some spare time, but I guess we won't get any. My face is really tanned from the sun and wind.

Will probably go ice skating this Saturday Night. Inside arena of course because the water around here never gets a chance to freeze.

My radio has broken and I took it down to a guy who repairs radios. He wanted 15 dollars to fix the thing and I told him no way. All it needs I think is a tube or two and I'll try and dig them up someplace.

Incidentally are there any more bottles of shaving lotion around the home. If there is would you please send me a bottle.

Strange as it seems I haven't ran short of cigaretts as yet. Always get Camels too but someday it will catch up with me I suppose.

Well I've been rambling along enough. I will finish for now and will write again next time when there is more to write about.

Beth has been writing regularly each day and I sure do appreciate it. She's really sweet.

Goodnight for now. Gotta go.

Love –
Ed

HYDROGRAPHIC OFFICE
WASHINGTON, D.C.

23 January 1945

Dear Mother –

Received your letter yesterday. Don't remember if I wrote and thanked you for the candy you sent. Opened them up at the office and passed some around. It was very good.

Glad you received and like the corsage. Didn't know if you would get it down at the store but I took a chance anyway.

It's only 9:30 A.M. now but writing this letter at the office before I start to work. Had a card party last night and feel a little tired what with staying up to about 2:00 A.M. this morning.

Last weekend I went down to Baltimore. Had dinner with a fellow and his wife who use to work in Massena. Stayed there till about 9:30 Saturday night then went to see the girl I use to know in Canada. I used her father's car this time and we had a pretty good time. The only thing that was bad is that I couldn't get a place to stay overnight because of the overcrowded conditions there. I finally took a 5:00 A.M. train Sunday Morning back to Washington and got to bed about 7:00 A.M.

Received a letter from Ed sometime ago. Think I wrote to you about it. Also one from Adeline and Mamie. Surprized to hear that Eddie has been discharged from the Army.

So the weather is bad and the temperatures low back in Buffalo. This is the mildest winter I have spent in my life. The wind is cold and sharp sometimes but never worse then what we have in Buffalo. As yet there hasn't been any snow to speak of and probably never will.

Pretty soon it will be time to go to the coffee shop for a cup of coffee but I will continue a little longer if I know what to write.

Incidentally, this camp is under Replacement & School Command or did I tell you that before? It sure seems strange to be on the other end of orders and regulations being issued.

We just got finished scrubbing the floor, a wooden one, and it looks clean enough to eat from. We used lye in the water and it bleached the wood.

How is the place without the kids? Pretty quiet? You can go visiting now that they are gone. There are a lot of people you should go and see.

Well this is the finish of the letter.

Love
Rum

31 January 1945

Dear Mother –

Just came back from bowling and bought some stationery while I was down there so I could write a letter.

Received a letter from Ed yesterday and answered it right away.

It's really been cold down here for the past couple of days. The wind is stronger then in Buffalo and tonight for instance the temperature is only 15° above but it feels worse then the 20° below in Massena.

It doesn't look like I'm going to leave Washington for sometime now. As you know I came here on temporary duty but that has been changed now and I'm here on a permanent status. Don't know how much it means but I suppose that Roosevelt won't have anything on me.

Went ice skating last Saturday at an indoor rink. The office held a party there. I sure don't know how to skate anymore. My ankles hurt like the devil after going around the rink only twice. Besides my girlfriend hadn't ever skated before and I had to drag her around too.

Don't remember if I told you or not but I took a trip to Baltimore 2 weeks ago. Saw a fellow and his wife I knew up in Messana and had dinner at their place. Then went to see the girl I knew up in Canada. Her father let me use the car which made it very convenient to get around town.

There are 15 sailors in our section now and 15 more from "boot camp" are coming in soon. This will double the section. Since we hardly do any work now I expect that when this new bunch comes in we can really rest.

As it is now we take an hour and a half for lunch besides having coffee in the morning which takes a half hour and coffee in the afternoon, also another half hour killed. Besides we kid around and talk for about another hour during the day. So you can see that life for me is pretty soft and at a job they can't even fire me from.

When this new bunch does come in, I don't know how soon, but when they do come the section will be split up into night and day shifts which will break the monotony and also give me a chance to get around Washington and be outdoors since summer weather is only 3 months away as far as this part of the country is concerned.

Also I'll be able to make it to Buffalo about once every 6 weeks without any trouble. The way its going to work, I'll quit at 5:00 P. M. on Friday and won't have to return to work till 5:00 P. M. Monday.

How is everything at home. Are you still working regularly? How is Freeman? Does he feel better lately?

Well I have rambled on long enough. I don't believe you answered my last letter if I'm not mistaken. Oh well. I'll probably get one from you tomorrow.

Love

Rum

P.S. It was just a year ago tomorrow that I left for "boot camp". What a difference tomorrow will be from that day.

"On Bivouac"

Tuesday
8:55 PM
13 Feb. '45

Dear Mother –

I'm writing this by candle-light, while lying down in my pup tent. WE have put two of them together, so we have more warmth. In this way we have 4 men in here. Of course, it's crowded, but quite comfortable.

We marched out here on Sunday, the whole battalion, 1,000 men and I was right in front with the three other squad leaders. It sure made quite a sight to see 1,000 men marching. We started at 8 AM and stopped every hour to rest for 10 minutes. At noon we had lunch, which consisted of sandwiches, sugar rolls and coffee.

We marched 16 miles. Sunday we had the most beautiful weather I've seen in a long time. We arrived here and first of all each man had to dig a foxhole. Then we put up our tents. The weather was just like spring. We had a few spiders & scorpions around but got rid of them.

Yesterday we awoke to find it raining very hard and all day was quite miserable, as we had to crawl in the mud under overhead artillery fire. Today was another beautiful day. We fired the machine gun again. I'm really learning how to fire all sorts of weapons.

Saturday another package of candy arrived from you. Yesterday they brought out here three packages, two from you & one from Mamie. I sure was tickled to get them, as something like that is sure appreciated in the bivouac. So far I opened the Betty Mor candy (2 lb. box) & they're delicious. I shared some of it with the fellows here in the tent & they too liked them.

Today they brought out Valentines from Mamie, O'Haras & you. Thanks. Also a letter (Wednesday) from you. Also letters from Betty & Harriet. And news from Wally. I'm enjoying this bivouac if only the weather holds out. We're supposed to go in on Sunday, but may go in sooner, maybe even Thursday, as some men will be sent out of camp and so all of the company will return to camp.

We get up each morning at 4:30 o'clock & march about six miles to where we fire our guns.

I'd better say goodnight & get some sleep, after I smoke a cigarette.

Had a letter from Major Ash on Saturday. He didn't have very much information.

Well, good night for now with best of

Love –

Ed

Sunday
7:05 P. M.
18 FEB. 1945

Dear Mother –

Well, here I am in Co. "C" 53rd I.T.B., where I transferred an hour ago. Have just unpacked and made my bed. I like these barracks much better as we have single beds instead of double-deckers. Also there are three stoves instead of two here. Also we're much nearer to the Service Club and Non-Commissioned Officers' Club.

We left the bivouac on Friday at 5:20 PM, in a drizzling rain, marching the 16 miles and arriving at camp at 10 PM. It sure felt good to take a hot shower. Yesterday we spent cleaning equipment and turning in some of it. Went to the new Sergeant's Club here last night and had a good time. Drank quite a lot of Budweiser beer.

I enjoyed the bivouac quite a lot when the weather was good, which was four out of six days. The Nazi Village fight on Thursday was interesting. We used real bullets.

I've figured out that we hiked close to 400 miles during the six weeks. I've had both pair of my GI shoes resoled.

The reason we Master, Technical and Staff Sgts have been transferred here is to take additional non-commissioned officer training. You see, this company is starting it's 3rd week tomorrow and we'll be with them for the balance of the cycle as acting instructors. It shouldn't be as hard as the first six weeks were. The privates, corporals & sergeants, who took training with us and finished yesterday, are going overseas. I made quite a few good friends among them.

We non-coms should have a little more time to ourselves now. Of course, we might have some studying to do in the evenings.

Some of the experiences which I'll remember from the bivouac are: shaving with greasy hot water which had been used for rinsing eating utensils. That's all we had & we had to shave.

Well, I've done it again! When we left for the bivouac a week ago I had a cold. Then on bivouac I wore wet clothes and wet shoes for two days, slept on the damp ground for five nights and at times was quite fatigued. The result is that my cold is <u>all</u> gone! If I were in civilian life I'd probably have double pneumonia.

Received your Thursday letter today. Also on Friday got the candy. Thanks a lot. I've got enough for awhile. Also they have candy for sale around here, once in awhile.

One thing about the bivouac which made me feel badly was that I lost the small metal crucifix which Al gave me on February 1, 1942, and which I carried in my pocket ever since then.

Yes, Beth has been writing again. She went to Atlanta for a few days so she didn't write then. Yesterday got a letter from Beth Rose, who is in Bermuda. She sent me a snapshot of herself. She still seems to be the most attractive girl I've ever been with.

I didn't know until I went to church this morning, that last Wednesday was Ash Wednesday. We had ashes placed on our foreheads this morning. They sure have a lot of dispensations in the Army. For instance, here we don't have to go to Confession but get general absolution, even when in mortal sin, and can go to Communion, if we have fasted from 1 A. M. The reason is that there's only one Catholic chaplain on the post. However, I always get to church on time and go to Confession. The general absolution is the same as they give on the battlefield when there would be no father for confession for thousands of men. The priest this morning said that we did not have to fast or give up anything for Lent as we've given up enough already. He comes out once in awhile and watches the men train, also on bivouac.

Well, I've figured out that my training will be finished on Good Saturday, which is the same as at Ft. McClellan 3 years ago. Wonder when I'll go there?

I'll say goodnight for now and go over to the Service Club for awhile.

Love –
Ed

A.G.F.R.D. #2
FORT ORD, CALIFORNIA

Sunday

1:40 P. M.
8 April 1945

Dear Mother –
Well, here I am, after the most wonderful and interesting train ride I've ever had. Arrived here this morning at 7 o'clock.

The reason the ride was so very interesting is because of the long stop-overs we had.

We left Camp Howze on Wednesday at 12 noon. Arrived at Forth Worth, quite a large city, at 1:30 P.M. Then we had off until 10 o'clock that night. So I got to see quite a lot of the town.

We travelled right across the whole state of Texas, so you can imagine how long that was. Then arrived in El Paso, which is right on the Mexican border. We weren't allowed to go into Mexico, as it's a foreign country and we needed special passes. So we just looked around El Paso. Stayed there for 4 hours.

Later travelled thru New Mexico and Arizona, covering quite a lot of desert. At times there wouldn't be any house or sign of civilization for 15 miles. The cactus out on the desert was sometimes 15 or 20 feet high. Just like trees. When we left Howze it was so cold, some of the men wore overcoats. It really got hot going thru the desert.

Incidentally, there were 50 of us travelling and we had 2 sleeping cars, which we kept at all times, even though we travelled via 3 different railroads, Sante Fe, Texas & Pacific, and Southern Pacific. You see, they'd hook our cars up to these trains. There were some civilians in the other cars.

Well, we arrived in Los Angeles at about 11 PM on Friday and were to stay there all night and leave on Saturday morning at 7 o'clock. We went out for awhile, but with the curfew we came back and slept in the train.

Then yesterday morning, the Colonel who was in charge of us, said that we wouldn't leave until 7 o'clock in the evening. So we all gave a shout of joy. A whole day to spend in Los Angeles!

First of all I grabbed a cab and went downtown and to a YMCA, where I took a welcome shower, after 3 days on the train. Looked around town for awhile, then took a street car and went to Hollywood. Hollywood is the same to Los Angeles, as Kenmore is to Buffalo, a suburb. I visited the famous Grauman's Chinese Theatre, where so many world premiers have been held. Also where famous starts have put their foot-prints and hand-prints in the cement. Bob Hope put his nose print there; Monty Wooley left an impression of his beard; Betty Grable left an imprint of one of her legs.

I stood at the corner of Sunset Boulevard and Vine Street, which Bob Hope so often mentions. Really many lovely girls in Hollywood. I saw such famous night clubs as Ciro's, Tracadero and the Brown Derby.

Then I took a bus and went up to Beverly Hills where all the movie stars live. It really is a beautiful spot, overlooking Los Angeles. I stopped in at the Beverly Hills Hotel, where there is a U.S.O. Then I got a map of Beverly Hills, which showed the location, with addresses of the movie stars. I walked around, looking at various homes, such as Loretta Young, Charles Boyer, Mary Pickford, etc. I'm forwarding the map in another envelope. Will you please save it for me?

It seemed rather strange to be walking and looking at all those movie stars homes. Some of them were right in a regular block, such as Loretta Youngs', and nothing to indicate that a movie star lived there. Others had high walls, swimming pools, etc. However, I didn't get to see any actor or actresses at all.

We couldn't go thru any of the studios, because of some strike which is on now, and about which you've probably read. Jack Benny has a small modest home.

I felt like going up, ringing the doorbell and saying "hello" but thought they might not appreciate it. All of Beverly Hills is very swanky looking. I sure would have liked to have stayed there a lot longer. It was very nice and warm, as a change from Texas.

We left L.A. last night at 7:30. It's about 350 miles from here, so I guess I won't be able to go there. Met a nice girl at the Beverly Hills U.S.O. and we danced for awhile.

Incidentally, the Colonel put me in charge of the 50 men who transferred here. We're all 1st, Tech and Staff Sergeants.

This is a beautiful camp and good 2-story barracks with showers and toilets inside. The Pacific Ocean is only about 1,000 feet from my barracks door. The nearest town is Monterey and we're about 150 miles south of San Francisco, where the big conference will begin on April 25th.

The address I've given you isn't complete, but I will have one by tomorrow when we get assigned to a company. However, you can use that one meanwhile.

We got a couple of shots today, and got brand new blankets. I guess we'll get final training here. I don't expect to be here longer than 2 or 3 weeks before going overseas. I had hoped to go to Ft. Meade, Md., but as the war there in Europe is almost over, we were shipped here. But I guess it doesn't make too much difference. I'm going to visit San Francisco if I get a chance. Probably next weekend.

I'm enclosing the orders; will you please save them for me?

Last Tuesday night I again went to see "The Clock", because I had liked it so much. I tried to find Judy Garland here, but no success. Of course, she may be in New York.

We're restricted in the barracks until 5 P.M. today in case they want to check us or our records.

The food here is the best Army food I've had since Camp Ritchie, Maryland.

I should be getting a lot of mail soon, as it's being forwarded from Howze.

There are now only 13 states in which I haven't been, and 6 of them are near home, the New England ones. The others are Oregon, Nevada, Colorado, Utah, Louisianna, Mississippi and Iowa. I have now see the country from one ocean to the other; and from the Canadian to the Mexican border. Five years ago I hadn't been further away from home then Watertown, N.Y.

Say, will you please look at the things I sent in that suitcase? I'm missing my sunglasses & also tobacco pouch and am wondering whether I put them in it by mistake. If so, will you please send them back? Thanks.

So long for now and I'll write again, soon.

Love –
Ed

NOTICE
CHANGE OF ADDRESS
9 APRIL 45

1ST SGT. EDWARD F. BARTZ 32212187
CASUAL. CO. 74 PLATOON 2
A.P.O. NO 15941
SAN FRANCISCO, CA.

1ˢᵀ Sgt. E. F. Bartz 32212187
277 Repl. Co.
APO 703 – c/o PM
San Francisco, Calif

Wednesday
1:50 P.M.
9 May 1945

Dear Mother –

Well, I finally received some mail today, 18 letters at once! There were your letters of April 9ᵗʰ, 11ᵗʰ, 12ᵗʰ and 13ᵗʰ; 2 from Mamie, one from Adeline, one from a Colonel in Birmingham, one from Elser, one from Beth (B'ham) (she'll be married probably this month); 2 from girls in Massena (one of them is a nurse in Ottawa, Canada); four from Peggy in Chicago and two overseas NEWS from Wally. So I sat down on my cot, lit a cigarette, (5 cents a pack) and spent most of the morning reading through it. It sure was wonderful to have that contact with my friends and loved ones.

I've been able to buy some tropical Hershey bars here. They don't melt like ordinary chocolates do. Also have Baby Ruth bars here. Ice cream, however, is unknown here. Incidentally, the hottest season here comes during April and May, so we're right in the middle of it now. Their rainy season will start. We had some rain the other night and when it rains it pours here in the Philippines.

By the way, I had a novel experience, while aboard ship, when we crossed the International Date Line. We crossed on a Monday evening close to midnight, so it immediately became Tuesday night, close to midnight; and in a few minutes it was Wednesday. So we skipped Tuesday. However, on my return trip to the U.S., I'll have the experience of going thru the same day twice. Say for instance, that we cross on a Sunday; the next day will be Sunday again, instead of Monday.

We sure were all glad last night to hear that the European War had ended. We listened to President Truman speak last night at 10 o'clock, (9AM your time). We have movies here every evening, out in the open, sitting on the ground under the palm trees.

We sleep in cots, inside of a tent housing 24 men. I know all the men, as we took training together at Camp Howze, and some I knew at Ft. Lewis. The meals aren't bad and there's enough of it. We drink coffee for breakfast and lemonade for dinner and supper. We have to do our own laundry, and can boil our clothes in an old oil drum. I take at least one shower a day and shave in cold water, but am getting used to it now. The water is quite soft.

The Filipino kids come around with cocoanuts, bananas and

hand made trinkets which they sell, but usually prefer to take a couple of packs of cigarettes.

Some native Filipinos here make a drink, tapped from the very top of the cocoanut trees, which is called "tuba". They say around here that two drinks will make one see pink elephants and have an effect like a sledge hammer blow in top of the head. No, don't worry, I won't touch the stuff. For one thing, I don't know what _else_ they put into it. I'll stick to water and an occasional can of grapefruit juice, which we can purchase at the PX.

We're able to keep very well informed as to the news; better than at Howze. We hear the news on the public address system 3 times per day. Also bulletins are posted in various areas. I'm able to buy my favorite news-magazine, TIME. It's a Pony Edition, about the size of a Reader's Digest, and no advertising. It's printed in Hawaii and costs 30 centavos, or 15 cents, same as in the States. By the way I read about 15 books while crossing the ocean. They had a ship's library where we were privileged to borrow books. Yes, it took a couple of days, or so it seemed, to get back my land legs after several weeks at sea. I slept out on deck several nights when it was rather warm below.

Just happened to think that this Sunday will be Mother's Day. I'll be especially thinking of you then.

My watch is running very well (knock on wood). Let's see, it's 3 years old now, I believe.

I'm enclosing a peso (worth 50 cents in U. S. money) which you might want as a souvenir.

Have my copies of YANK started coming as yet? If so, have you looked through any of them? You might find them interesting.

Well, so long for now, Mother. I'll write Adeline & Mamie one of these days. Take care of yourself.

Love –
Ed

1st SGT. EDWARD F. BARTZ
CO. M 164th INFANTRY REGT.
FOUGHT IN PHILIPPINES
AND ENDED UP IN JAPAN,
NEAR TOKYO AFTER THE
SURRENDER.

Thursday
9:50 AM
10 May 1945

Dear Mother –

Last night I received two more letters from you. One was dated April 16th, and sent to Ord. The other was April 22nd and addressed to APO 15941. Some of the men here yesterday received letters dated the 29th and 30th of April.

I'm enclosing a letter which we all received upon boarding ship. Will you please save it for me.

They're going to have the movie "Keys of the Kingdom", which I saw at Howze, however, I liked it quite well so will go see it again tomorrow or Saturday night.

This morning I heard something moving around under my cot so I looked and found a little monkey scampering around.

You've no doubt received my War Bond for May, by now. It should be for $50.00, and so should all the subsequent ones.

The Filipino kids here call all of us soldiers, "Joe" and they're always looking for candy or cigarettes, but give something for exchange such as bananas, cocoanuts, etc.

Well, I guess I'll say so long for now. I sure do hope that you're not worrying about me, as I'm both well and happy.

Love –

Ed

Sunday, Mother's Day
9:50 A.M., 13 May 1945

Dear Mother –

Went to Mass this morning, for the first time since Easter
Sunday at Camp Howze. Received Holy Communion. Found out that
we don't have to fast at all, but can go right after breakfast. However, I
didn't know about it so I fasted.

Have been getting some more mail. Yesterday received letters
from you, dated April 3rd & 4th, sent to Howze. Also received letters
from Peggy dated April 19th & 29th.

At Mass we observed both Mother's Day and victory in Europe.
There were several Filipinos at Mass, as you no doubt know that many
of them are Catholic. They were converted by the Spaniards 400 years
ago.

Received a letter from Rum, which is the one he mentioned to
you that he'd write, thinking I was still in the states.

I hardly ever dream but the other night I dreamt about Father
Lutz. It seems I was walking along, in Buffalo, and met him on the
street.

Sunday here is like any other day except for church services in
the morning.

It's now 10:10 A.M., and back home it's 9:10 P. M., last night,
and you'll soon be going home from work. I suppose you don't have any
of my letters yet, so I hope you're not worrying.

I wish I could send you some flowers for Mother's Day, but I'll
make up for it the next time.

You've probably heard about the point-system which has been
established for demobilization of the Army. Right now we had a stag
party for the 2 guys who are leaving for Pearl Harbor last Monday.
Everybody drank plenty of beer and seemed to enjoy themselves very
much.

Youhave to have 85 points to apply for a discharge, but
the level will be lowered from time to time. I have 40 points now.

I'm glad you got to see Bob. I haven't seen him for 3 years now.
Maybe I'll meet him out here somewhere, who knows?

Have you seen any good movies lately? I went to see "Keys of
the Kingdom" Friday night and sat in the rain watching it. Of course, I
was wearing my poncho so didn't get wet.

So long for now, Mother, and all my love to you on this your
Day!

Ed

Am enclosing a stick of chewing gum wrapped in <u>tin</u> <u>foil</u>!

Roman E. Bartz, Sp (X) 3C
Hydrographic Office
U.S. Navy
Wash (25), D.C.

16 May 1945
c/o Air Nav.
10:00 P.M.

Dear Mother –
Received the package you sent today. It arrived very quickly,
you must have sent it out Monday and it came early this morning. The
things were wrapped up similar to Christmas presents and I didn't
know what was in any. Everything was in good shape, where did you
get all of those chocolate candy? Thank you so much for everything.
Came back from bowling about an hour ago. It took about that
long to unwrap the things in the package. It was the last time for the
season and I'm glad because it has been hot here for the past 3 days.
We put on our whites just in time because the temperature has been in
the 90's. The whites feel cool and clean compared to the blues. Went
bowling in my civilian clothes however.
Just walked around last Sunday after calling you. You didn't
sound very cheerful. Which I could do something to stop your worrying
but there isn't anything that you don't already know. Received a letter
from Daniel a few days ago. All of his letters take at least 3 weeks
before they reach me and don't forget that Ed will probably travel for
about 3 or 4 weeks, so you can expect a letter during the 6th or 7th week
and not before then. So you can really stop worrying and look at it from
a practical viewpoint.
Had a letter from Eugenia Gafih today. She is still working for
Spence Lens and not doing much in particular.
My girlfriend and I are invited out for drinks over to one of the
Chiefs' place tomorrow and Friday we have another ballgame. We won
the last one 3 to 2. I pitched, but was lucky to win.
That's all for tonight and thanks for everything.

(unsigned)

28 May 1945
8:00 P. M.

Dear Mother –
 Received your letter today and also one from Mamie. Had a
letter from Ed again Saturday. That is the second one I have gotten from
him since he is in the Phillippines.
 The package you sent came Friday. Everything was in good
shape. Have enough candy to last me a year now. Thank you very much.
 Saturday was my day off but the weather was miserable. It
started raining about noon Saturday and didn't stop until Sunday
evening. There was a fine mist all the time. Otherwise the weather has
been quite cool and I have been wearing my blues in the evening when I
go out though it is against regulations.
 Saw a night ballgame between Washington and Cleveland last
Thursday.
 Same thing at the office. No change in work or hours or stuff
like that.
 Starting raining about 20 minutes ago and there is a real storm
up.
 Will write to Ed tonight and probably some others too. It's a
real good night to catch up on my correspondence. Have to get more
stationery however. Told a fellow to get some for me, hope he did.
 There really isn't anything to say so I had better quit.

Love
Rum

1st Sgt. Edward F. Bartz 32212187
Co. "M" 164th Infantry
APO 716 c/o Postmaster
San Francisco, California

Wednesday
6:20 PM
Phillippines
30 May 45
Decoration Day

Dear Mother:

Haven't as yet received any mail since my arrival on this island, but I'm still hoping that it'll soon be here.

I'm using the portable typewriter which we have here in the company headquarters tent, where I sleep and work.

There isn't very much to write about, that is anything which would pass the censor.

We've been having hot weather, cool nights and daily showers which usually last for just a few hours. I've been eating pineapples, bananas and papayas. The papaya tastes something like a melon, but grows on trees. It has a slight pepsin taste.

Tomorrow is Corpus Christi Day, which is not a holy day of obligation in the States, but is elsewhere, therefore here in the Philippines I'm obliged to attend Mass.

Being out in the field like this we don't buy cigarettes or candy, but get an issue about every five days of cigarettes, tropical Hershey chocolate bars, soap, toothpaste, shaving cream, blades, gum, etc.

Incidentally all the fellows with whom I trained at Howze and who came over with me, have all been split up in various divisions and regiments.

Let me know whether YANK magazine has started coming in at home and whether you've glanced through them. I should be getting my copies of YANK, LIFE, TIME & Reader's Digest sometime within the next two months, I hope.

I suppose that my $50 war bonds have started coming in, by now and that the allotment is coming in regularly.

Have you seen any movies lately? Of course, I haven't since my arrival here.

So long for now and hope that the next time I'll be able to write a more interesting letter.

Love –
Ed

What You Buy With WAR BONDS

From primary trainer planes, airmen of the Army and Navy are graduated to advanced trainer planes, larger and in some cases, multiple motored. Advanced trainer planes for the Navy cost about $46,000.

Training in these larger planes is the last step before the pilot is skillful enough to handle the giant bombers and multi - motored torpedo planes. Our aviators must have the advantage of the best training equipment, for air superiority over our enemies is essential if we are to win this war. Your purchase of War Bonds and Stamps will give them this advantage. Invest at least ten percent of your income in War Bonds every payday.

U. S. Treasury Department

St. Joseph's Church
Varysburg, N. Y.
Postmarked
May 31, 1945

Dear Friend, Mrs Bartz,

Thank you very much for your favor. Assuring you that your generosity has been deeply appreciated, with sincerest best wishes to you and yours, hoping to see you soon, I remain,   I have lighted the vigil light, as you requested. Fervently shall I remember your dear son, Edward, at the Altar. May God ever bless and protect him!

Fr Lutz

Sunday
8:50 A.M.
3 June 45
Philippines

Dear Mother –

Well, as I write this you should be going home from work in an hour and 10 minutes, last night.

Haven't had any mail for over two weeks now, but no doubt it'll all come in one large batch.

This is really beautiful country around here. We're on a plateau and look down over the hills. The nights, as I mentioned, are really cool and the days aren't bad.

I wrote Mamie about putting in an article in the NEWS. Will you please send me a copy of it when it appears. Thanks.

The Red Cross has a tent set up here, where they give out cookies, stationery, etc. Of course, there are no women connected with it here. Did you ever get to see the picture "The Clock"? I'm sure you'd like it.

Are they going to have a family picnic at St. Mary Magdalene's this year? Did you do anything special on Decoration Day?

Well, I'll be saying so long for now in order to get this out in the mail.

Love –
Ed

Friday June 8, 1945
2030

Dear Mother —

Received your letter a couple of days ago. Had one from Ed yesterday too, and also from Adeline. Think I'll do some letter writing tonight. Have at least 10 letters to answer and maybe I can do it tonight.

It has been really cold down here for the past few weeks. Been wearing my blues in the evening all the time.

Went to the cinema last night. Didn't care for it very much. It was the same stuff over again and the seats were very uncomfortable.

Had Wednesday off but it was cool and cloudy all day so I didn't get to go outdoors much.

We got a 45 cents a day raise in subsistence which makes it $3.00 a day now. My promotion didn't come thru however but they can hang themselves so far as I'm concerned.

We get guard duty about twice a year. Just stay in the building to take phone calls, etc. It is a very easy job and not like boot camp.

Haven't played ball in a week's time now as we weren't scheduled.

Don't know if I should split my vacation up or not. For every 5 days leave I get 2 days travel time. One of the fellows wants me to go up to Maine with him in October. He lives there.

Sure haven't much to say. Ed probably has a lot more to tell then I ever will.

That's all for now —

Love —
Rum

Thursday
Philippines
14 June 45
7:00 P. M.

Dear Mother –

Have moved along and we're in quite a nice spot now. Have a small stream nearby where we can bathe.

It's strange how one loses track of dates under conditions like these. I have to stop and think, before writing, as to what the day and date are, instead of knowing them automatically.

I've been eating quite a few items which I hadn't had before, such as preserved butter, which doesn't melt; dehydrated potatoes, carrots, etc.; eaten cereal which all it needs added to it is water (really good cereal, too). Also made coffee using cold water only. This is all necessary so many times hot water isn't available.

As yet my mail hasn't caught up with me. Once it does get straightened out, however, I suppose I'll get quite a stack of it in the first mail, as the whole month of May has to be accounted for.

Have you heard whether Daniel Rusgaj had returned from Europe or not? I suppose he writes to Rum once in a while.

How's everything going at the store? Do you still work every other Thursday night? Tell Estelle "hello" for me.

How's Freeman getting along at work? I suppose he still has irregular hours and, no doubt, quite busy now, what with the railroads shipping everything to the Pacific Coast.

It's raining right now and I'm filling up my steel helmet with rainwater, with which to wash tomorrow morning.

I'm getting quite tan from my waist up, and am feeling very well.

Attended Mass last Sunday, which was held out in the open, under a tree.

We were fortunate and each got an issue of six (6) bottles of Ballantine's beer, which had come over. It really tasted good, after more than two months. Cooled it with rainwater.

Well, I'll say goodnight for now. Take care of yourself.

Love –
Ed

18 June 1945
9:00 P. M.

Dear Mother –

Haven't had much of a chance to write lately but
tonight I decided to do so. Received your letter today. The airmail letter
came last week. I forgot what day it was.

The package arrived last Thursday. The oranges were alright.
The bananas weren't too bad but slightly soft. The cherries were moldy
except for a few. Don't know what happened to them. Might have been
wet or gotten damp somewhere. The nuts are good and still have some
left. Thank you for everything. It has been very hot here for over a
week. The temperature has been 95o everyday and the humidity makes
it exceptionally warm and uncomfortable. The precipitation just keeps
rolling off me all day even though I work without a jumper. Have to put
on a clean uniform everyday.

Went out to the River yesterday, wearing my civilian clothes.
Took the girlfriend out boating. We stayed out all day. Got quite a tan
while out there.

Last Wednesday I slept at the office because I was a guard for
the day. It wasn't had and I enjoyed it very much, being a break from the
routine.

General Eisenhower came into town today. Most government
workers got the day off but we didn't. Probably have to wait until
some Admiral comes back from the wars. Right now I am listening to a
rebroadcast of his speech to Congress today.

I will start my vacation around July 4, I'm not sure as yet but
I will be home on that date and stay for at least 12 days. Your best
bet would be to start your vacation about July 8 or somewhere around
there. I haven't a calendar so I don't know the exact dates.

What you really should do however is to go someplace on your
vacation instead of staying home. Not while I'm at home of course.

My writing is getting worse all the time. I can't even read it
myself sometimes.

This coming Saturday is my day off. Would like to take a trip
someplace but don't know where. Too hot to go to New York. Well
that's about all for now.

Received a letter from Daniel last week. He is still in Germany
and doesn't know when he is coming back.

Thanks again for the package you sent.

Love

Rum

(Opened by U. S. Army Examiner)

Saturday
Philippines
9:15 A.M.
23 June 45

Dear Mother –

Well, here I am in a hospital. Nothing to worry about though. We had moved to another island and I was taken ill there. It was diagnosed as amoebic disentery and I was flown by an Army plan to this island to be hospitalized. Aboard the transport plane there was an Army nurse and she was the first woman I had seen since leaving the States, and it sure seemed good.

I also enjoyed flying again. It was the first time since January 1944 when I flew from B'ham to Buffalo. The Pacific sure looked blue below us.

This hospital is made up of many large tents. Each tent is a ward & there are plenty of Army nurses here. They all wear slacks. It sure seems good to sleep on a cot, with a mattress, pillow and <u>sheets</u>. Have also had my first ice-cold water and <u>bottled</u> <u>coke</u>!

I feel quite well now but have to remain here until I'm cured of disintery. After that I'll go back to my old outfit.

The last boat trip was quite rough and I got sick for awhile.

Now that I've moved my mail will again be delayed. I think I would just about have received some. In order not to mix things up too much please keep sending your letters to the same address, at Co. "M."

Just to show you what a small world this is: One of the fellows in my company also from N.Y. State (New York City) was on another boat and got to talking to one of the sailors who also was from N.Y. State. This fellow mentioned to the sailor that another fellow, meaning me, was from N.Y. Then the sailor told him that he had taken "boot" training with a Bartz from Buffalo, last year at Sampson. So that was Rum! I didn't get to see the sailor or I would have asked him his name.

Also here in the Philippines, have met a soldier from Buffalo, who lives on Box Avenue near Moselle.

I am now allowed to tell which island in the Philippines I'm on. It's _____ , the _____ by Americans _____

I was here before, then went to Miridanao and then CEBU and now here again.

I'll say so long for now and will write again soon.

Love –

Ed

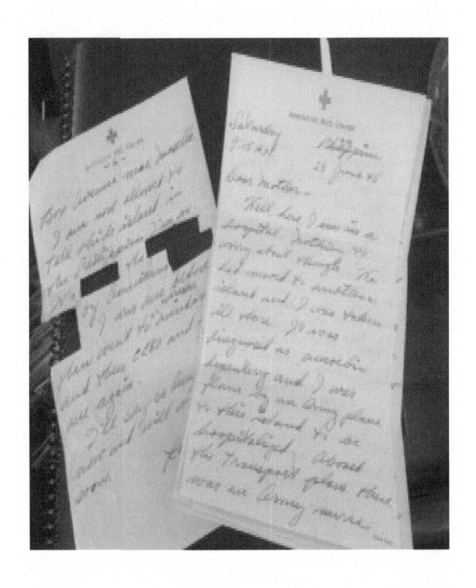

Letter censored by the Army.

(Opened by U. S. Army Examiner)

Sunday
10:35 A.M.
8 July 1945

Dear Mother –

Yes, I'm still in the hospital but feel OK. I'd like to be back with the company. Having 170 men under me does give me a sense of responsibility.

Still no mail.

We had a little entertainment at the Red Cross the other night. A Filopino band furnished the music and it's surprising how well they can play our popular music. A Hawaiian girl danced the hula and she was pretty good.

When you get the chance to send me a package will you please send the following items, which I haven't been able to get:

1. Vaseline Hair Tonic
2. After-Shaving Lotion (either Yardley's or Old Spice, if possible)
3. After-Shave Powder (same as above)
4. Shaving Cream (They have brushless only here).

I guess you'll have to show them this letter at the Post office before you can send me a package.

Well, so long for now. With good luck I'll probably get the package for my birthday.

Love,
Ed

(Opened by U. S. Army Examiner)

Monday
1:20 P.M.
LEYTE, P. I.
9 July 1945

Dear Mother –

Well, here I am again. We've received six bottles, or should I say cans, of SCHLITZS beer, except for some patients who are not allowed to drink. It sure tastes good. Also got some pretzels and cheese crackers.

In one of your letters you mentioned that you were not going to the movies for the duration. How come? I'd feel happier if I knew that you were enjoying yourself, instead of sitting around and worrying. After all there's nothing to worry about. I've got a good job in the headquarters of the company and have a good bunch of officers and men. I get plenty of good food, cigarettes and beer and am happy, considering that I'm on the other side of the world. I think you'd enjoy pictures like "The Clock", etc.

You asked whether 0500 was 5 A.M. Yes, that's right. I wouldn't be surprised if the Army and Navy time weren't adopted after the war. They've already made some watches like that. Here's the way the time runs:

0100 is 1 A.M.	0700	1300	1900
0200	0800	1400	2000
0300	0900	1500	2100
0400	1000	1600	2200
0500	1100	1700	2300
0600	1200	1800	and 2400 is midnight

All that is going around the 24 hours. Now it's 1340, which is 1:40 PM. I took a walk down to the beach and looked at all the Navy boats out there. Plenty of sailors around flirting with the Filipino girls, like we all do. Some of them are very pretty and speak good English.

Well, I'll say so long for now. Take care of yourself and don't worry about me.

Love –
Ed

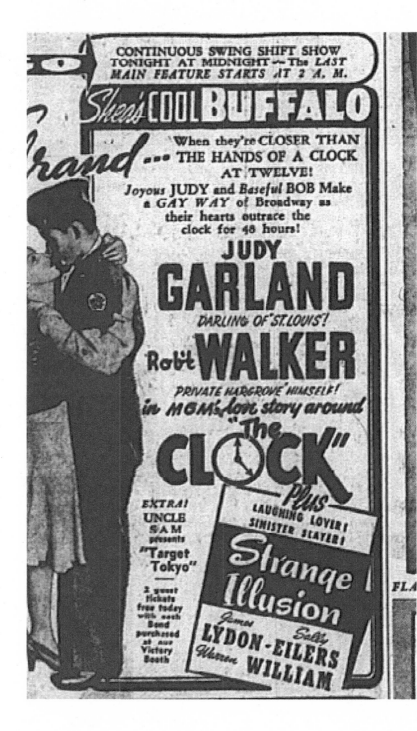

(Opened by U. S. Army Examiner)

Friday the 13th
LEYTE, P.I.
July 1945
9:45 A.M.

Dear Mother –

Day before yesterday I received six more letters, making a total of 55 in four days. Two were from Al; one from you, one from Rum, one from Mary Szwanka and one from my mail clerk. Although our company is on the next island, his letter took seven days to reach me. Some of my letters have been reaching you in that length of time.

I guess I never told you about the type of work I do as a First Sergeant.

Well, first of all if we stay in any one area for any length of time we put up our Headquarters tent, in which I stay with four men on my staff. There's my mail clerk, who also does other clerical work; there's my messenger; a radio & communication man; and finally a telephone man. The telephone man at once strings a line to battalion headquarters and thus connects me also to the other companies in our battalion, "I" "K" and "L". Our battalion letters spell this word out. The 1st bn. has "A", "B", "C" and "D". The 2nd Bn. has "E", "F", "G", and "H". For some reason the letter "J" has never been used for a company in the Army.

Then my field desk is set up. It's about twice as long as my footlocker at home and is like a large trunk. It is set up on a stand and the lid opened. Inside the desk I have a portable typewriter. Also various records and books, which I use for company administration. I have a folding Chair, which the Japs left behind on one of the islands. It still has Japanese writing on it. I also have Japanese staples.

Every day I have to make up a morning report and send it to Bd. Hq. In the report I record any changes in our personnel, such as men going to the hospital, or coming out of one. Any transfers or additions are recorded. Also if anything unusual happens I make a record of it.

Then the men who want to go on "sick call" are recorded by me in a "Sick Book" and the men are sent to the dispensary, where the doctor determines whether the man goes back to duty or the hospital.

I also have to make out various details such as K.P., guard duty, and work details.

In the morning I fall in the company of 170 men. Then the platoon sgts report to me as to whether everyone is present. Then I "about face", salute the Captain and report to him.

In other words I more or less run the company, as the Captain is too busy with other work. Many times he'll tell me what he wants done, and I get in touch with my three platoon sergeants (Tech. Sgts).

You see, I look out for the welfare of my men and am sort of a link between the Captain and the men. I really enjoy the job. I have more responsibility now than I ever had in my life and that should help me in civilian life.

Well, I guess that's all for today. I'm enclosing a Philippines peso.

Love –
Ed

(Opened by U. S. Army Examiner)

Saturday, 9:45 A.M.
14 July 1945

Dear Mother –

Yesterday received eight more letters, making 63 in six days. I've read each one at least three times. These last letters were all old ones, four of them being sent to Camp Howze, and the others to 277th Co., and my APO while at sea. One letter was from you, one from Adeline, from Rum, Mrs. Boyer in Massena, T/Sgt. O'Regan at Ft. Lewis, one from Peggy, one from Mrs. Johnson at Columbus, Georgia and one from DiPasquale in Germany.

You remember me telling you about DiPasquale, don't you? He was my roommate at Benning and was nervous about going overseas. He was a Staff Sgt., but now is a sergeant first-class. The letter from Mrs. Johnson was dated April 25th. She was my secretary at Benning. She's expecting a baby sometime this month.

Sgt. O'Regan was a good friend of mine at Lewis. He's in a hospital there, with arthritis in his shoulder. He's 37 years old. He and his wife want me to visit him in New York City after the war. Mrs. Boyer used to be my landlady in Massena.

Your letter was dated May 3rd. Adeline's, or rather the O'Hara kids, sent me a Father's Day card. In your letter you mentioned that Rum had been home and flew back to Washington.

We have regular showers here at the hospital, same as in the States, except that we have cold water only. However, that's good enough as it's quite hot here. It's a known fact that shaving with cold water toughens the beard, so the barbers are going to have quite a time when all the soldiers come back. I shaved my beard and mustache off, as the nurses didn't like it too well. There's one nurse here who is a Croatian and she's real cute. She understands and speaks some Polish.

We get eggnog to drink every day and they serve it ice cold. Real good. It's made from powdered milk, and fresh eggs, and tastes alright.

Well, I'll say so long for now.

Love –
Ed

(Opened by U. S. Army Examiner)

Monday
P. I.
12:35 p.m.
16 July 1945

Dear Mother –

Yesterday I received 14 more letters, making a total of 77 in eight days.

Four were from you; two from Al; one from Adeline; two from Peggy; one from a Massena girl, one from Mary Szwanka, one from a friend at Ft. Ord and one from a fellow right here in the Philippines.

This last one was a surprise to me, more or less, as I wrote to him at Ord and he's here now. His name is Sgt. Lenard, a Polish boy from Pittsburgh. We took basic training together at Ft. Lewis and then were transferred to Camp Howze and later to Fort Ord. However when I sailed, he stayed behind.

He's in the Infantry, with the _____ Army, and I believe, on Lugon. Maybe we'll get a chance to see each other.

Incidentally, once in a while I get a letter from someone, who says: "So you're in the South Pacific." The fact is that I'm <u>not</u> in the South Pacific, but in the <u>North</u> Pacific, as we are north of the equator. However, this area is usually referred to as the "Far East".

Your letters yesterday were dated May 14th and 27th; also June 23rd and 25th! So my mail is now beginning to come in more regularly.

I sure was surprised to hear about Dr. Borosgewski dying.

Incidentally when I sent you the pictures of various divisional insigne I forgot to explain what ours stands for.

The stars represent the Southern Cross, a formation which appears in the sky in this part of the world.

The Southern Cross is to us, what the North Star is to you all in the U.S.

I didn't go to the movies last night as it rained & they're outdoors. If I had my poncho (raincoat) here I would have gone.

Heard over the radio that there's still fighting on Mindauno.

Well, I'll say so long for now.

Love –
Ed

(Opened by U. S. Army Examiner)

Tuesday
8:05 A. M.
17 July 1945
P.I.

Dear Mother –

I hope that it doesn't rain tonight as they're having a pretty good movie – Bette Davis in "The Corn is Green".

However, on Thursday night I'm going even if it does rain. The picture then will be Greer Garson and Gregory Peck in "The Valley of Decision". I read the book at Fort Lewis and really liked it. It's about a family in Pittsburgh, just after the Civil War until Pearl Harbor. Greer Garson is my favorite actress. She plays the part of a servant in this picture. It's a brand new movie too, as I read about it not very long ago.

I was looking at a map of the world, and figured that I could travel either East or West from here, and the distance to New York City, by water, would be the same, a little over 11,000 miles. Going West I'd go through the Indian Ocean, up the Red Sea, thru the Suez Canal, across the Mediterranean Sea and cross the Atlantic Ocean.

Going East, I'd go across the Pacific Ocean, thru the Panama Canal and up along the Atlantic coast.

As I said, we're 13 hours ahead of the U.S. East Coast; and 16 hours ahead of California. You see, the day starts here and goes across Asia, Europe and the Atlantic, to the U.S.

You mentioned that Ronnie was four weeks on the Pacific. I still don't <u>where</u> he was. Do you?

Well I'll say so long for this time.

Love –
Ed

(Opened by U. S. Army Examiner)

Wednesday
1:55 P.M.

18 July 1945

Dear Mother –

Well, they stopped treatment on me today. Now I get a 10-day rest period and after that laboratory tests, and if they show that I'm cured I'll go back to the company. If not I get more treatments. I've been here four weeks today. When I had pneumonia at Benning I stayed 17 days.

We have a parakeet here in the ward office. It's a species of parrot; this one is green. It seems quite tame and doesn't fly very far away from here.

Saw "The Corn is Green" last night, but it was rather dull.

Well, our Navy and Air Corps is really hammering away at Tokyo and Japan. Those Japs should give up, if they know what's good for them.

The way it looks now I should be back with the company shortly after Aug. 1st.

Haven't received any mail since Sunday but they haven't given out today's mail as yet.

Incidentally, I wanted to mention to you that you don't have to write every day to me. I can imagine that it's sometimes inconvenient, or else hard to find something to write. You needn't worry about my not getting enough mail, as I have a lot of friends writing to me.

Well , so long for now.

Love –
Ed

Thursday
0945
19 July 1945
P.I.

Dear Mother –

Yesterday we had a U.S.O. show, which had 3 American girls, just from the States. It sure seemed good to see an American girl, wearing a dress, instead of slacks.

Incidentally, when I go walking along the road, and come across some Filipino girls, they say "Hello, Joe". So I smile and say "Hello, Josephine" and that seems to tickle them.

I don't see how these girls can carry large bundles on their heads, without hanging on to them. It really gives them a graceful carriage, though.

Well, tonight I'm going to see "The Valley of Decision," and hope it'll be as good as the book. The book was about 900 pages long.

As I haven't had any mail since Sunday I expect I'll get some this afternoon.

Haven't heard at all from the girl in Birmingham. She's probably married by now.

In one of his letters Al mentioned that he had gone down to the harbor to see an LST boat. I've already been on an LST, an LCI and a Higgins boat, in addition to the Army transport on which I came across.

Well, good morning, for now.

Love –
Ed

(Opened by U. S. Army Examiner)

Friday
1605
20 July 1945
Leyke, P.I.

Dear Mother –

Went to see "Valley of Decision", last night and liked it very much. It was changed quite a lot, that is they shortened it, from the novel. The picture covered only about 10 years, whereas the book covered about 70 years. However, the picture was still good. Greer Garson is my favorite actress.

I'm enclosing a 10-centavo piece, which is worth 5 cents in American money. We also have 5 centavo pieces, 20 and 50. 100 centavos make 1 peso.

Well, so long for now.

Love –
Ed

(Opened by U. S. Army Examiner)

Philippines
Monday
0940
23 July 1945

Dear Mother –
    This morning we were moved from one ward to another. This one is much nicer. We have hospital beds, instead of cots. Also the floor is concrete, instead of bare ground.

    Went to see "Molly & Me" last night and it was a pretty good comedy.

    Guess what? They're going to show "The Clock" this coming Thursday. I'm going to see it for the third time. Saw it twice at Camp Howze. I guess I'll never get tired of seeing that picture.

    I should be getting some more mail soon.

    As I write this you're probably at Adeline's.

    So long for this morning.

Love –
Ed

P.S. I am enclosing a 2 peso bill.

(Opened by U. S. Army Examiner)

Tuesday
1005
24 July 1945
Philippines

Dear Mother –

At present I'm reading a very good book. It's "Brave Man" by Ernie Pyle. Last year I read his book "This Is Your War", which also was very good. In both books he mentions that he has more respect for the Infantry than any other branch of service. He lived with the Infantrymen for quite awhile. In "Brave Men" he has some kind words for the First Sergeants.

He sure went through a lot, for a man who did not have to be there and who could have stayed very comfortable in the States, if he wished to do so.

He's the one who started the movement which made Congress pass a bill giving the combat infantrymen $10 per month extra. It wasn't so much for the money that the Infantrymen wanted this, but for the special recognition they'd receive, and appreciation for what they did.

It sure was a great loss for us soldiers when he was killed. I heard about it at the time I was coming overseas. It saddened us all, following so closely the death of our Commander-in-Chief.

So long for this morning.

Love –
Ed

St. Joseph's Church
Varysburg, N.Y.

Postcard Post-marked
July 26 1945
5 PM

Dear Friend – Mrs. Bartz,
   Thank you very much for your favor. Assuring you that your
generosity has been deeply appreciated, with sincerest best wishes to
you and yours, hoping to see you soon, I remain, I have lighted the
vigil candle as you requested. That all may go well with your dear son,
Edward, is my fervent wish and prayer. Kindest regards.

Fr. Lutz

(Opened by U. S. Army Examiner)

Philippines
Friday
1845
27 July 1945

Dear Mother –
    I went to the "The Clock" last night and enjoyed it as much as the first two times.
    Before the movie began they played some classical recordings over the loud speaker.
    They played a lot of pieces which I like, such as Tschaikowsky's "Piano Concerts in B-Flat Minor", Grieg's "Concerto", "The Warsaw Concerto" and Libelin's "Finlandia."
    The latter one reminded me of the World's Fair, when they had that All Nations Lagoon, with fireworks and played "Finlandia." That was five years ago this month.
    No mail for almost two weeks now.
    So long for now.

                        Love –
                        Ed

(Opened by U. S. Army Examiner)

Philippines
Saturday
1440
28 July 1945

Dear Mother –

Last night they had a Quiz Contest here at the Red Cross. There were two teams, the Americal Division and the 81st Division. There were three men on each team.

I was one of the three on the Americal Team. We won and each one of us got 12 packs of cigarettes.

This noon for dinner we had fresh peaches. That is they were the frozen kind.

Really were good with the ice still on them.

I weighed myself this morning and I tip the scales at 172 pounds.

Some new nurses, about 18 of them, arrived here fresh from the States. They were still wearing their woolen uniforms. Most of them look like school girls. They had just finished their nurses' training and came into the Army. In the evening they fixed their hair in pigtails and looked like school girls.

They haven't distributed the mail for today, as yet, so I don't know whether I have any or not.

Well, I'll say so long for now.

Love –
Ed

Boys in New Guinea Grateful For Smokes Sent From Home

Letters Just Received Tell of Plans for Christmas Celebration in Far-Off U. S. Outpost

Smokes "give me pleasure" and "movies are almost the only other entertainment outside reading old magazines," writes Private First Class John Leland from somewhere in New Guinea.

His letter is typical of many received from service men far and near who have received cigars or cigarettes through the Buffalo Evening News Smokes-for-Soldiers Fund.

Many New Year greeting cards continue to arrive. Some men send formal thank-you cards, adding their own postscripts of gratitude. Others seem to get the reportorial spirit when writing to a newspaper and so they describe places and events concerning them.

Grateful for Gift

Private Leland's letter from New Guinea continues:

"The carton of cigarettes you sent arrived here a few days ago and I am grateful for them, not only because they will give me pleasure but because thoughtfulness and generosity in behalf of us who are far from home console us by showing that we are not forgotten.

"Life here is so different from that we left that we appreciate any evidence of interest in our welfare, since as long as such interest continues we are assured that when we do come home we will not come as strangers.

"Even our letters are not so much accounts of personal experience as attempts to preserve our individuality in the minds of others. We do not regard gifts in terms of cash, thoughtfulness may be considered, but efforts in terms of the impulse which prompted the giving, and it is for that I thank you most.

Not in New Guinea

the New Year—and thanks for the smokes."—Private Frank Cuviello.

Tough Assignment

Here are excerpts from other recent letters:

U. S. MOSQUITO FLEET—"I appreciate your generosity and thanks a worldful. I don't smoke cigarettes, but I do smoke a pipe. I shared my gift with my mates that weren't so lucky. I'm now in the roughest, toughest outfit the Navy's got—the PT's. And from here, gentlemen, I give you my thanks. It's good to hear that good old Buffalo is doing its bit to keep the boys supplied with smokes."—A Western New Yorker, Leonard D'Iugos.

SOMEWHERE IN AUSTRALIA.—I have just received a carton of cigarettes with your compliments. I wish to express my deep appreciation for such a fine act. I am stationed in a desolate part of Australia and the only people I ever thought knew I was there were the Japs who visited us quite frequently. The cigarettes certainly came in handy.—Staff Sergt. Joseph A. Weigel.

NORTHERN IRELAND.—I wish to extend my most sincere thanks for the cigarettes. Since receiving them things have been moving very fast, and now I find myself somewhere in Northern Ireland. You've no idea how much pleasure we get from the cigarettes you send us. It seems like a string that helps keep the ties to home that much stronger. Ireland in itself is very beautiful and I wish everyone could see what I have seen.—Corporal Howard Cronk.

COLUMBIA, S. C.—The smokes you sent are all gone now, so I just filled in the card you enclosed. When I get some cigarettes from you again I'll have to be more care-

(Opened by U. S. Army Examiner)

Thursday
1015
Philippines
2 August 1945

Dear Mother –

It looks as if I'll be leaving the hospital very soon, maybe tomorrow.

I'm enclosing a 50 centavo piece, which is worth 25 cents in U.S. money.

No mail as yet. Can't understand why the delivery has been so erratic. Probably when I return to the company it'll be normal.

I sure have read a lot of books here. Incidentally, I had my eyes examined. My right on is 20/20 which is perfect; my left one is 20/15, which is better than that.

Well, so long for now.

Love –
Ed

6 August 1945
9:45 P.M.

Dear Mother –

I'm on guard duty right now. Have to sleep here tonight too. The watch starts at 4:30 P.M. and ends the following morning at 9:00 A.M. It's quite easy however and I don't mind it too much.

Went to Baltimore last Wednesday, my day off, and visited the girl from Alaska. Had quite a good time. Yesterday took a trip to Chesapeake Bay which is about 50 miles from D.C. Had my first swim in salt water. Didn't care for it very much. Rather have the fresh water.

Have received the letters you have been sending. Got the last one sometimes last week.

My roommate left last Thursday for Pearl Harbor. I bought the other half of the furniture, so now I own the whole works. While I have the apartment by myself, you could come down and visit me if you would like too.

Going to start working evenings for a civilian who is a carpenter. I'm going to do the painting for him. I don't know anything about painting but he says there is plenty of money in it so I'll take a stab at it for awhile.

Have received 2 letters from Ed lately. One dated 16 July came a week before the other dated the 14 of July.

It has really been raining around here for the past 2 weeks. I never seen anything like it before. All rainfall records for the month of July were broken. Hope it eases up soon, because it has rained just about everyday and plenty hard too.

I'm going to look pretty dirty tomorrow because the uniform I have on now I wore to the beach yesterday and I can't get home to change it. That's all for now.

Love –

Rum

Tuesday
7 August 1945
0840
Philippines

Dear Mother –

Well, I left the hospital yesterday and am here at a casual camp, several miles away, awaiting transportation to my outfit. May be here several days.

Had a good time at the swimming party last Sunday. The ocean was as warm as bath water. Of course, the water was very salty and stung the eyes. The Red Cross girls went swimming with me. Later had tuna fish and egg sandwiches, ice cold lemonade and cookies.

I was surprised yesterday to see some white civilians, ranging in age from three to 60 years old. Then found out that it's a refugee colony, and they're awaiting transportation to the States & Europe. Quite a few pretty girls.

Didn't receive any mail the last day at the hospital, so there must be a stack of it for me at the company.

So long for now.

Love –
Ed

Cebu,
Philippines
Aug. '45

Monday
9:00 P.M.
18 September 1945
TOKYO, JAPAN

Dear Mother –

I just came back from the movies. Saw "Animal Kingdom" with Ann Sheridan & Dennis Morgan. Really liked it. The Theatre is really nice. It felt good to sit on regular seats, instead of the ground or in cocoanut logs. I sat in a section, which is reserved for officer and Master & First Sergeants. Could see very well from there.

This morning , at 5, when I awoke the sky was all red and I thought there was a fire somewhere. The wind was blowing very hard. Later we were warned that a typhoon would hit us at 6 o'clock tonight, but fortunately it did not materialize.

I received several letters today. Two were from you, one the 7th & the other the 9th, postmarked the 10th, only 8 days ago. Also came a letter from Mamie, dated MAY 5th! It was sent regular mail to my ship's APO. It seemed strange to read it. Mamie said "looks like the war with Germany will soon be over."

No, you need not send the LIFE magazine, but can save them. I'm enclosing a first page from YANK, printed in Tokyo. Also another clipping.

Today is a typical fall day and I love it. I see where you're going to have Standard Time again, after almost four years. Then I'll be 14 hours ahead of you.

Also came a letter from Rum today. He mentioned about his promotion. Makes $200 & more per month. I get $180 but do not have any expenses.

Well, goodnight for now. It's going to be a swell night during which to sleep.

Love –
Ed

Wednesday
8:30 PM
19 SEPTEMBER 1945
TOKYO, JAPAN

Dear Mother –

Now that we're out of combat I thought we'd stay put once we got here, but we're moving in a few days. It's only a half mile away, but it's always a headache for me when we move, as I have so many different things to attend to. This I think will be the last move, however. Anyway, we're moving into better buildings and I'm glad as this one would have been quite cold this winter, in fact it's quite cold now.

I'm enclosing a news sheet and have marked out something of interest. Now that it's been printed I can tell you that when you read that the Americal Division was fighting on Mindanao, it wasn't the whole division of 15,000 men, but just our battalion about 800 men. We were part of the 108th RCT (Regimental Combat Team). We were really outnumbered as there were about 5,000 Japs opposing us. Of course, we had the better equipment and air support. It seems strange to see that we were mentioned in the Buck Rogers strip. Did you see it in the News?

Did I tell you that I got 5 points for a battle star for the Philippines? That's in with my 53 points.

I can also tell you now that all those pineapples I ate on Mindanao I picked on the Del Monte pineapple plantation, which they owned before Pearl Harbor. I guess I'll have to send them a check for all the pineapples I ate.

Well, that's all the news for this time. Good night, Mother.

Love –
Ed

SUNDAY
8:00 AM
23 SEPTEMBER 1945
TOKYO, JAPAN

Dear Mother:

Yesterday I received your letters of 27 and 31 August, although a few days ago I received yours of 7 and 9 September. I guess that these last ones were delayed because of our move here to Japan.

I'm enclosing an Americal newssheet, in which appears a reprint of the September 8th issue, in Tokyo Bay. You'll notice the article about the Americal being the first infantry division to land in the Land of the Rising Sun only preceded by the 11th Airborne and the 1st Cavalry.

Say, will you please send me about three athletic supporters. I have one old one, but never wore it in the Philippines because of the heat. We're going to have training in the mornings, and all sort of athletics and sports in the afternoons. Also please send me a sewing kit.

I guess my portable radio broke because of all the exciting news which came over it; just couldn't take all that excitement.

I sure was surprised about Retta coming in to the store. How did she look? Also was surprised about Betty working in the Deaconess. Wonder what she looks like?

I enjoyed reading the articles about Springville and Sardinia.

Also enclosing a post card which I got from one of the kids here. I guess someone in his family must have received it from a Jap soldier stationed in Manchuria, as it has that postmark on it.

Today is a really truly fall day, cloudy and cold. We're going to get our woolen clothing in about a week.

Well, I guess that's all for today. So long with best of love.

Ed

27 September 1945
9:00 A.M.

Dear Mother –

Received the box of candy bars you sent last Friday. Where did you ever get all of them? Also your card came yesterday. Thank you for both.

Haven't heard from Ed lately. The mail must be tied up again. Had a letter from Daniel last week. He is now in Austria. Has 68 points but doesn't know when he is coming back. Probably will be soon now.

Papers are full of articles telling of discharging men from the Army but the Navy never has a thing. They sure are slow about doing something. It doesn't make much difference to me if I have to be in for a little while longer. Still think something may come up during the early part of next year.

Been working almost every evening. Didn't work last night but will tonight if I don't get guard duty because my turn has come up again. I am a standby and if some of the others are gone I will have to take the place of the missing man.

Has been very warm lately and I hope it cools off before Monday when we put on our blues.

There isn't really much to do around the office. Nobody seems to work too hard.

Well that's all for now.

Love
Rum

Friday
9:00 PM
28 Sept. '45
Tokyo, Japan

Dear Mother –

Have received your letters of 5 and 12 September. Also one from a girl in Massena, dated MAY 16th, and sent to Camp Howze Texas! In it she mentioned that the weather was still pretty cold and that they had occasional snow flurries – and here it'll be winter once more.

Well, I've been busy packing and getting ready to move. Tomorrow morning we're moving into that building a half-mile away. It'll be much better. Now I hope I won't have to move again until I go home.

I guess I won't be asking for any more packages as they'll probably arrive after I've sailed for the States. Anyway, you can send the ones I requested thus far. So far I have not received any.

I expect to be home in January, if not sooner. Please have a couple of bottles of beer for me in the refrigerator. Also some <u>milk</u>! I wonder what milk tastes like? Also ice-cream.

Well, goodnight for now, with best of love,

Ed

Saturday
2000
6 October 1945
TOKYO

Dear Mother –

Received today your letter of 26 September. Also two from Mamie, one of which she wrote last Saturday, only a week ago.

Well, the rains have stopped and it's quite cold now. The typhoon never did hit us. That's the second time we were warned, but it never came.

I was quite busy today, otherwise I would have gone into Tokyo. Well, that's all for tonight.

Love –
Ed

Sunday
2125
7 October 1945
TOKYO

Dear Mother –
 This sure has been a busy day for me. Didn't seem like a Sunday, except for the fact that I went to church this morning. The chaplain has a little room, alongside the chapel, where the Blessed Sacrament will be exposed all this week. It sure does bring a touch of home to me.
 We had a delicious supper tonight consisting of fried chicken, canned corn and apple pie. All we needed to top it off was French fries and ice cream.
 Also got an issue of cigarettes today. On Tuesday we will get an issue of American beer, and I'm looking forward to it. At least here it'll be cold and not like in the Philippines.
 Am enclosing an article from the "Stars and Stripes," which I think is quite interesting.
 Well, that's all for tonight, with best of love from

Ed

Monday
1820
8 October 1945
TOKYO

Dear Mother –
Didn't go to Tokyo today as it rained again. I'll try tomorrow again.

Am enclosing some more clippings. There hasn't been any mail for a couple of days as all planes have been grounded. Should be a bunch of it when it does come in.

Things are about the same here. The barracks are improving in appearance.

Well, good night for this time with best of love,

Ed

TUESDAY
2125
9 OCTOBER 1945
TOKYO, JAPAN

Dear Mother:

I just came from the movies and guess what I saw? It was
"A Song to Remember". I certainly did enjoy, and I believe it'll be on
tomorrow night and I'll go to see it again. The music and acting was
really wonderful, especially his playing of "Polonaise". You haven't seen
it, have you? I know that you mentioned that Adeline & Butch went to
see it; also Mamie mentioned seeing it again. I've been humming and
whistling different Chopin tunes since I left the theatre.

It rained today again so didn't go to Tokyo, but am glad that I
didn't as I would have missed the picture. Remember how I tried to see
it all over the U.S., and here I finally see it in Japan.

There haven't been any letters for several days now, and I'm
enclosing a clipping which'll explain the reason. However, today arrived
your package, mailed 16 August, and containing nuts and soap dish.
Thanks a lot; those nuts will come in handy as tomorrow we're getting
a dozen cans of American Beer, apiece. Also did appreciate the soap
as I'm almost out of it, and it's hard to get. I thought I'd have to start
washing with laundry soap which they have in the kitchen here. Say,
could you send me a couple of batteries for my Army flashlight, also a
bulb. The flashlight is about the same as the Boy Scouts have. You could
send them First Class and I'd get them probably within two weeks.
Also today came 4 SEP's which you sent in July. Of course, the reason
I received the package & magazines is that probably arrived in Japan
about a week ago, but delivery on that mail is slower than letters.

Am enclosing also some other clippings. Well, I guess that's
about all for this time. Goodnight with best of love,

Ed

PS: That sure is a fancy soap dish and I really like it.

THURSDAY, 11 OCTOBER 1945
TOKYO, JAPAN

Dear Mother:

In a way I'm glad that the planes have been grounded and
therefore we're not getting any letters, as in that way the postoffice
is finally getting around to delivering packages which they have had
stuck away in some corner for weeks. Today two more packages arrived.
One from you and the other from Elsa. Yours was sent July 24th and
Elsa's also in July. Your package contained the "T" shirts, pajamas, soap,
toothpaste and Vaseline hair-tonic, all in perfect condition. Thanks a
lot for everything. Of course, now I need flannel pajamas, but I'll wear
these until I receive them.

The package from Elsa was all banged up and wet; apparently
having been in the rain somewhere. She sent packages of gum, gum
drops, two rolls of film, stationery and greeting cards for me to send
out. The gum drops were all gooey and the film pretty well banged up
and rather wet, but the heavy wax paper around it may have saved it. I
hope so.

Yes, I went to see "A Song to Remember" again last night and
enjoyed it even more than the first time.

It finally stopped raining tonight after about 4 days. Yes, it's
pretty cold. Yesterday we all got shots against influenza. I never know
that they shots against it.

I did receive one letter yesterday, from Peggy, dated October 2nd.
Don't know how it got through.

We had steak and cherry pie for supper tonite. Really delicious.
Yes, we'll be getting turkey for Thanksgiving Day, my 4th one in the
Army. (I mean my 4th T-Day)

Oh yes, also arrived my first copy of YANK, dated 17 August,
so my subscription must have started. Also arrive 2 LIFE's from you.

I now know about 30 words in Japanese and can talk pretty well
with the Japs. I've always been able to pick up language pretty well, such
as French and Spanish in high school.

Well, Mother, goodnight for this time with best of love,

Ed

PS: Am enclosing a regimental newspaper.

Postcard

12 Oct. 1945
12:10 A.M.

Dear Mother –
     Left D.C. at 7:00 P.M. Thursday. Had one stop so far at
Columbus, Ohio. Next stop is Kansas City at 1:00 A.M. The ride is very
smooth so far. Will be in Los Angeles sometime this morning. Hope to
get some warmer weather out there.

Love

Rum

Postcard

12 Oct. 1945
1:30 P.M.

Dear Mother –
    Still flying. Will be in San Diego in about 2 hours. Made a
stop in Amarillo, Texas early this morning. About a half hour ago we
landed in Phoenix, Arizona. It sure was hot there. Expect to get to San
Francisco in about 6 hours.

Love

Rum

12 October 1945
12 Midnight P.C.T.

Dear Mother —

Just a short letter because I'm quite tired and sleepy after 25 hours of flying.

Left Washington 7 in the evening 11 October and arrived here 7 in the evening 12 October. Here meaning San Francisco.

We got ourselves rooms in downtown San Francisco. It is a real bustling town. Will try and see some of it tomorrow if we don't leave. There is a possibility that we won't be able to get a plane until Monday.

Stopped in Los Angeles long enough to refuel and that was about all.

The flight down to Frisco was very smooth. You ought to see all the sailors in this town. Guess there is a sailor for every other kind of person in town.

Well I hope to stay here until Monday but if I don't I'll write from Pearl Harbor as soon as possible.

The past 2 weeks really have been moving for me.

That's all for now —

Love
Rum

Roman Bartz

AIR NAVIGATION OFFICE
PACIFIC OCEAN AREA
N.A.S. NUMBER 29
c/o F.P.O. SAN FRANCISCO, CALIF.

18 October 1945
Honolulu

Dear Mother,

I sent out a letter last night and I made out a Money Order today which I want to send so I decided to write again. There really has not been anything new since yesterday. Swimming is not too good right now because it looks like the rainy season has started. I was all set to go swimming this noon when down came a terrific shower which lasted about a half hour and then it stopped. So that rained out my swimming. Right now it is pretty nice—the sun is shining but it gets dark in about an hour and the wind is pretty cool after the sun sets. Incidentally, I am dictating this letter so I am not putting anything too personal in it. The guy who is taking it down is quite a gossip.

I might go swimming or take in a movie tonight or maybe drink some beer. So far I have been drinking beer every night since I came here, which is about the best pastime you have in the evening. I have not seen a movie yet but most of them are cowboy pictures or some sort of a picture you have never heard of before except the movie producer.

So far I have not received any of your mail but Betty sent one yesterday and I got another one today. She wrote them, however, the day after I left Washington. The mail service will start flowing in pretty soon, though.

I sent a letter to Ed. I wonder if it will go directly to him or whether it will go all the way to Frisco and then to him. It would be practical to send it directly to him if you can, but you cannot tell what they will do in a case like that.

I had better quit now because it is a little after four and it is time to go home such as you call home and this guy who is taking this down in shorthand wants to type it up yet and he probably wants to scram too.

So write soon,

Love,

Rum

MONDAY
2030
22 OCTOBER 1945
TOKYO, JAPAN

Dear Mother:

The barracks tonight are as quiet as a tomb. Yesterday we had 145 men here in the company. This morning 103 of them were transferred out, leaving only 42 of us, so you can imagine how very silent it is here. Out of the 42, 31 of them will leave with the Americal Division about a week from now. They have 60 or more points. I won't be going with them as I have only 53. The reason I'm staying behind is to get everything set for the movement back to the States. I'll no doubt be working day and night for the next week. Then when I get everything all set, I'll be transferred out. Dirty trick, isn't it? But that's the Army and I'm used to it. There are 10 other men with me who will stay until just before the division leaves. They're also helping me out.

I got my orders tonight, but will not leave for several days. I'm being transferred to the MP's, which makes me mad. During the wartime when it would have been a soft job, I was in the infantry, and now in peacetime I get an easy job. Of course, it's only for a month, so I'll not kick too much about it. I have my address so when you receive this, use the following address, as I'll be there by then:

720th MP Bn
APO 503 c/o PM
San Francisco, Calif.

I don't know exactly where it is, but I'll soon find it out. It's not supposed to be very far from here, probably near Yokohama.

Received letters from Adeline (the 11th) and Peggy today. Also a cut Halloween card from the O'Hara kids. Incidentally, there's a Japanese town here on Hanshu, called Ohara.

Am enclosing some clippings from the Stars & Stripes.

This place is still up in the air as far as the closing date is concerned. Nobody seems to know what is going on but most of the fellows are eligible for discharge now that the new point system has come into effect. I am still hoping to be home by January or so. Although this climate will be pretty tough to leave.

Goodnight for this time, with best of love

Ed

PS: You'd better not send any of the pictures which you'll have developed. I'll send them to Peggy, etc. when I get home. On second thought, please send me just one set of each just so I can see them. Thank you.

They had the rosary here at the chapel tonite and I attended.

23 October 1945
Honolulu
10:45 A.M.

Dear Mother –

Received your letter and card yesterday. Thank you. May I repeat, put down Air Navigation Office on the address instead of Navy Air Station. This way the mail won't go all over the place because it is quite large.

Well it's after one o'clock now. Went out for a 2 hour swim. I didn't bother eating because I have been doing too much of that lately. I feel like I have put on about 10 pounds in a week, what with 3 big meals a day and beer. The water was very warm today. There is a seaplane takeoff area right in front of the swimming area and the planes are continually taking off. It's quite a sight to see those heavy clumsy looking things take off.

Expect to take a trip around the island over the weekend and see what the rest of the place looks like. The other side of the island has more vegetation such as pineapple trees, cocoanut trees and other jungular growth.

Received 5 birthday cards from Adeline today signed by the kids and Milton, rather their names were on them.

Haven't done much work today. I'm quitting at 3 o'clock today to take care of some things. Really in the office about 5 hours a day.

Expect to hear from Ed soon because it's over a week since I've written to him.

Betty writes everyday, so I get at least one letter a day.

Guess I'll quit now and write a letter to Mamie because I haven't written to her as yet.

Love

Rum

25 October 1945
2:00 P.M.
Honolulu

Dear Mother –

Received your letter of Sunday 21 October today Thursday. The days are moving a little faster now that I have been out here several days. At first they really dragged but now I have the hang of things around here and I like it a lot better.

However the way things look right now I wouldn't be too surprised to see you in about 3 weeks. The officers are checking the equipment now to see what to take back and how much space it would take on a ship. If we fly back it would be really nice. There's nothing definite as yet if this office will close down but the Hydrographic Office in Washington has told us to be ready to leave immediately. This needs the approval of the Chief of Naval Operations however and that's what we are waiting for. The notice should come sometimes before the 15th of November, and then we shall know.

The weather around here feels just like Washington in mid-summer. It's really hot and doesn't cool off any in the evening. The days are just average. That is it gets light about 6:00 A.M. and is dark at 6:00 in the evening.

This is the only paper I have at the office and it isn't too good. I have seen quite a few movies lately. There isn't any place to go in the evening as far as sightseeing is concerned because it gets dark too early. I expect to take a trip this weekend however.

Haven't heard from Ed as yet.

The swimming is really ideal around here and I go out on the beach just about every noon hour, for about 2 hours.

That's about all for now.

Love
Rum

28 October 1945
9:30 P. M.
Honolulu

Dear Mother —

Received your letter of 23 October this morning. It was Sunday but I went down to the office for awhile to get the mail and its better to stay there then the barracks. Played a couple of games of chess and read.

It rained most of the day and is quite cool tonight. Looks like the winter weather is setting in around here.

Took a trip to the other side of the island this afternoon. Went both ways by jeep. Crossed a mountain about 6000 feet high and the road really had some curves in it. Never had a ride like that one before. It was the most scenic one I ever had. Enjoyed the whole thing very much. Mailed a cocoanut from the other side too. You should get it in about 3 weeks time.

Received 2 letters from Ed last Friday. They both had been mailed to Washington. One told about his trip to Tokoyo.

The meals are pretty good out here. Yesterday was Navy Day and we really had a feast. Had turkey, cranberry sauce, mashed potatoes, peas, fruit salad, grapefruit juice and apple pie with a half of pint of ice-cream. Could hardly move after eating all that. Had steak for dinner today and fresh eggs for breakfast. Only powdered milk around here but there is plenty of ice-cream and that is very rich. Have scrambled eggs for breakfast once a week but they aren't too good because they are powdered eggs.

That's about all for tonight. Will write soon again.

Love

Rum

Wednesday
1325
31 Oct. 45
TOKYO

Dear Mother –

This morning I received Adeline's Xmas package, mailed Oct. 2nd. It sure was welcome & had two rolls of film. Also came 4 SEP's from you; a Readers Digest, thru subscription & 2 YANKS. One of the SEP's had an article about the battle of Antwerp, Belgium & and colonel who commanded the city during the siege. There was a picture of him, too. It was Colonel Gullatt, who was Rum's boss in Massena, same as Captain Sibley was mine. Col. Gullatt was a Major in Massena. I've written Rum & sent him the clipping.

Well, tomorrow the regiment boards the ship for the States & I'm still here. Haven't been told to leave as yet.

Saw a good movie last nite. It was Ernie Pyle's "G.I. Joe". Was quite realistic.

Well, so long for this time, with best of love –

Ed

Tuesday
12:15 PM
13 NOV. 45
TOKYO

Dear Mother –

This is my lunch hour and I thought I'd write you as I haven't
for several days now. Have just received your letter of 3 Nov., the
first one addressed here to the MP's. I'm glad to hear the rolls of film
arrived OK. I hope they'll develop OK, as I'm afraid the tropical heat in
the P.I. may have ruined them.

I went to the Rodeo at Meiji Stadium here last Sunday and
really enjoyed it. It was a perfect fall day and there were 55,000 soldiers
there, American mostly, but also some British, New Zealanders,
Australian and Russians. Also British sailors.

I got a thrill out of seeing over 100 planes come over the
stadium; sure made a roaring noise.

Our Co. "D" barracks burned down to the ground last Sat. nite.
I'm forwarding copy of the newspaper Starts & Stripes. On page four
you'll see a picture of the fire. Only 30 minutes before it was taken I
was in those barracks (mess hall) eating my supper. I never did finish
it. I thought for awhile that our Hg. Barracks would catch fire, but the
Tokyo Fire Dept. came and sprayed our building. The sparks fell like
snow all over the place and I wore my steel helmet.

You'll also see a write-up in the S&S about the Rodeo and the
Lt. who rode the Emperors white horse. It sure is a beautiful animal.

One of the men who got burned in the fire on Saturday, came
with me from Co. "M". The silly fool ran back into the burning building
to get his <u>GUITAR</u>! It takes all kinds of people I guess. Nothing was
saved at all. The 170 men were moved into other barracks 5 miles away.

I've been dancing downtown but I guess Adeline showed you
the letter I sent her.

So long for now with best of love –

Ed.

THURSDAY
2010
15 NOVEMBER '45
TOKYO

Dear Mother –

Received today your letter of 5 November, so now the mail is coming in within ten days.

Yesterday I sent you pictures of some shoulder patches. I wonder if you could get me some at the Army & Navy store. If possible please get 3 Americal and 3 8th Army. It seems strange to have to write to the States for them but we don't have them here. We, who were in the Americal Division, can wear that patch on the right shoulder, and the 8th Army on the left.

It might be easier for Mamie to get them. There's an A&N store (on Eagle, I believe, I'm beginning to forget the names of the streets). Anyway, it's just across the street from Ulbrich's side entrance, and she knows where that is. You could send them right in an envelope.

It seems strange how you can't always believe what you read in the papers, or hear over the radio. You said you heard that the Americal sailed several days early. Actually, they sailed a week <u>late</u>.

Also about the items that all soldiers in Japan have hot showers. We still take ice-cold showers and the temperature is near freezing. Of course, the officers have <u>hot</u> showers.

Well, goodnight for this time.

Love –
Ed

I'm enclosing clippings. Also program of Rodeo, which I attended last Sunday. Please save it for me.

Friday
1947
16 Nov. 45
TOKYO

Dear Mother –

Well, "C" company had some hot showers put in & so I took one today and it sure felt good. I'm sitting here in my room, smoking my pipe and have a cozy fire in the stove. It's pretty cold outdoors and it seems good to be here.

I guess I forgot to mention before, that there were photographers from various magazines at the Rodeo, so you'll probably be seeing pictures of it. I saw LIFE's cameraman there. Of course, there also were the newsreel men taking moving pictures.

Remember early in August I wrote and said that we were in the 6th Army? That was because the 6th was going to invade Japan and we of the Americal would have been the first to go in. As soon as the war ended we were put back in the 8th Army.

There's a rubber plant in front of our building. I should say a tree, as it's 20 feet high. Anyway, the leaves are the same as we had on our plant at home.

Well, I guess that'll be all for tonight.

See you soon, with best of love –

Ed

P.S. I guess the reason it took so long for Rum's letter to get here is 'cause he addressed it c/o Postmaster, San Francisco. It went to the States and then here. I'll have to tell him to address it just "APO 201 – U. S. Army" and it'll come direct. I suppose the same will be true of my letters to him.

Sunday
1300
18 NOV 45
TOKYO

Dear Mother –

Well I'm not going home next month either. The new system goes into effect December 1st. The low score will be 55 points, and I have 53, so I'll miss out by 2 points.

Any soldier having 4 years of service as of December 1st will be eligible to get out of the Army. I will be 2 months short. So it's 2 short either way.

I'm enclosing clipping in regards to the new system.

I suppose while I'm here I might as well make the best of it.

So long for this time.

Love –
Ed

Monday
2015
19 NOV. 45
Tokyo

Dear Mother –
Have just come from the movies where I saw a swell picture.
It was "Captain Eddie", life story of Rickenbacker. It begins when the
plane he's in, crashes in the South Pacific in October 1942. Remember
the story about them drifting around in the rafts? It was in LIFE
magazine. Have you seen the picture?
Speaking of movies, did you know that Olivia de Havilland,
the actress, was born here in Tokyo in 1916? So was her sister, Joan
Fontaine, in 1917.
Well, I guess that's about all for this time.
Goodnight with best of love –

Ed

Tuesday
1940
20 NOV 45
TOKYO

Dear Mother –

Well, I finally received some mail today – 5 letters and a Thanksgiving card from the O'Haras. The letters were from Peggy, Mrs. Johnson, Mamie, Adeline and you. Yours, Mamie's and Adeline's all had about how worried you were in regards to Rum, and then that he called up from Washington.

I guess Rum and I <u>have</u> been causing you a lot of worry since we went into the Armed Forces. Well, we'll soon be home to stay.

I'm enclosing some more clippings, one of which is a map of the invasion that was to take place. You'll notice that we were supposed to hit the island of Kyushu in Japan. The 8th Army wasn't to go in until Spring 1946, that's why we were put in the 6th. Please put the map in my scrap-book.

Rum sure had a short stay in Hawaii. Any chance of him getting out of the Navy now?

Well, that's all for tonight, with best of love –

Ed

Friday
1830
23 NOV. 1945
TOKYO

Dear Mother –

Well, we moved today. I rather thought that we would since "D" Co. barracks burned down. We're still in Tokyo, but about 6 miles from downtown. However, the "EL" station is only a block away so I can get down in no time. There sure is a lot of noise when those trains go by. I'll get used to it though, just like in New York.

I like these barracks much better than the other ones. I again have a private room, with another soldier. However, this room is twice as large as my other one. Really nice.

Received this afternoon, your letter of 12 November, where you mentioned about Rum & Betty being home.

There goes another "EL" train. It almost seems as if I were at the YMCA in New York City.

Incidentally, in the S&S, which I sent you yesterday, there was article about Thanksgiving Day on the front page, and where various soldiers were asked what they had to be thankful for. Some answered "Nothing", as you probably noticed. They're the ones who just came over and had no hardships, not even the heat of the equator. I sure am thankful that we didn't have to make the invasion of Japan during wartime. Also thankful for many other things, having good health, knowing that you're alright, etc.

Well, I'll say goodnight for now, and finish straightening up my new room here.

Best of love –
Ed

P.S. – I hope my next move is home, but that was what I said the last time. This is the 5th different place in Japan for me.

Saturday
1 December 1945
TOKYO
1931

Dear Mother –

Received this morning your letter of 20 November. No, I didn't receive the clipping about Rum going to Hawaii. I guess that was a letter you sent to the 164th. I'll get those eventually, I guess you had sent all the snapshots there, too, right?

I went to Yokohama this afternoon again, to the 8th Army. It was a beautiful day so I enjoyed the ride. Stopped at the Red Cross Canteen there for some hot coffee & doughnuts, served by Japanese girls.

Well, today the 55-point men are eligible to go home, but, of course, that doesn't mean they'll be going home very soon. There are many 60-pointers left in Japan yet.

We each got a half-case of American bottled beer, and I got "Budweiser" one of my favorites.

Well, so long for this time, with best of love,

Ed

Monday
1845
3 Dec. 45
TOKYO

Dear Mother —
    Received today your letter of 24 Nov. Yes, I'll get all those snapshots you sent, although it may not be until I'm home.
    You mentioned about Rum getting more pay than he expected. There are two reasons for that 1) 20% increase for overseas duty. 2) Flying while on mission of duty. Any soldier or sailor who, in performance of official duty, use aircraft, get so much an hour more for the additional risk be takes.
    Personally, I think it's safer in a plane, than in a car or bus. Of course, ships and trains may be safer.
    You said you received a "large nut" from Rum. I presume that it's a cocoanut. You see, cocoanuts on trees look different than you see there in the market. They have a thick covering, which later is taken off.
    On Mindanao we had the natives climb the trees and pick them for us. Then we cut off one end with a machete, and drank the milk, which really tasted delicious.
    You see, we've had nothing but chlorinated water since coming overseas. Even here in Tokyo.
    A few times on Mindanao when we were in such a position that we had no water, we filled our canteen with muddy creek water, then put 4 Halozone tablets in it, waited 30 minutes, then held our noses and drank the water. In that tropical heat I drank about gallon a day. Because the bombing has damaged so much of Tokyo's water works, the water has to be chlorinated, before being fit to drink. I'm used to it now after 8 months.
    Well, you answered one of my questions — you received the sketch of me. Now, did you get the Jap hata (flag)?
    Enclosing picture of Co "D" barracks fire.
    G'nite for tonite with best of love —

Ed

This Japanese flag was actually found on the ground in Japan by Edward while on maneuvers with his battalion. He had each man sign and annotate it with the city/state they came from prior to sending it home to his mother. His daughter had it framed for him to hang in his office.

Wednesday
2050
5 Dec. 45
TOKYO

Dear Mother –

For some reason the mail has slowed down again. Haven't had any at all for a couple of days.

I found a photo shop near here and took one of my rolls of film to be developed. Will get the pictures back in five days. I still have one more roll to take.

Have been keeping pretty busy lately, with all the new men coming in.

I'm enclosing a couple of clippings from yesterday's Nippon Times.

The weather is still continuing cold and a stove here feels good.

I forgot to mention before, I had to turn in my Army wristwatch when I left the Americal. Since then I've been wearing my own watch and it's keeping pretty good time, tho it no doubt needs a cleaning. After all, I wore it during that Infantry Training at Camp Howze. Also on Leyte, Mindanao & Cebu. You gave it to me in Spring 1942.

Well, goodnight for this time, with best of love –

Ed

Saturday
2130
8 Dec. 45
TOKYO

Dear Mother –

Well, the mail is really coming in for me. Received letters from Major Ash, Mr. Peters, Bette from Georgia, and yours of 27 November with the shoulder patches enclosed. You don't know how very much I appreciate having those patches. I took them right over to a Jap tailor, and had them sewed on my Eisenhower jacket, shirt and field jacket.

Today, also, we got some more clothing: another shirt, two jackets & an overcoat, but I guess I can get patches for them when I return to the states.

Went to Mass this morning as it's Immaculate Conception. We have a Polish chaplain, a Lt. Rynkowski.

Still keeping pretty busy here and haven't had a day off in 2 weeks, not even a Sunday.

As you mentioned in your letter, I don't mind staying here a little while longer as I'll get more of a chance to see this strange country, which I'll probably never visit again.

I'd like to go to Mt. Fujiyama & perhaps go skiing. It's 60 miles from here.

You mentioned about the "Nippon Times" being expensive as it costs 35 sen. 200 sen makes one yen, and a yen is 6 ½ cents, so 35 sen is about 24 cents, making the "Nippon Times" 1 cent cheaper than the "Buflo News".

Major Ash expects to get out of the Army next month. He's got over 51 months service, which is what officers need, or 73 points.

Mr. Peters mentioned about Mr. Choun dying.

Beth said her husband is in Wake Island, with the Navy.

Well, g'nite and thanks again for the patches.

Love,

Ed

Sunday
2100
9 Dec. 45
TOKYO

Dear Mother —

    Received today your letter of 29 Nov. So the snapshots came out alright. I wish you would have sent me one set of each roll. Will you please send them to me now? I'll probably be here all of January and I'd like to see them. The two pictures of me, with the monkey, were taken on Cebu, about three days before we sailed for Japan.

    Yes, I received the patches yesterday, as I mentioned in my letter. Sure do appreciate them.

    Had a pretty good time tonight. The Tech Sgt who rooms with me and I went downtown in a jeep. Went to the American Red Cross. They are located in a swell building near the Emperor's Palace. There are thick rugs all over the place and large mirrors.

    Guess what? They had some Japanese girls there who make recordings of voices. So I made a record for you; the other side is for the O'Hara kids. The trouble is that it's a breakable record, but I'll pack it in some wood box and mail it. It's a Jap record and they play the other way around, that is, they start in the middle. I don't know how it'll work on our American phonograph, but you can try it and see.

    I'm going to enjoy myself here as much as possible while I'm here in Tokyo.

    I'm enclosing a clipping from today's paper, which I think is pretty good and true.

    Well, that's all for tonite and please send both sets of snapshots.
               Love —
               Ed

P.S. The kids in one of those pictures are Japs, taken when we first landed in Japan.

Saturday
2020
15 Dec. 45
TOKYO

Dear Mother –
 Still keeping pretty busy in my dual capacity as 1st Sgt and
Personnel Sgt. Major. They're really making me earn my pay.
 I'm enclosing some negatives. I already send you the pictures so
you need not develop these.
 In another envelope I'm sending you a 1946 calendar printed
by the Japs here. Also on it are Jap-English words & phrases; they
work across the page. For instance "O-ha-yo" means "good morning"
"Arigato" is "Thank-you". That's the phonetic spelling.
 Well, that's all for this time I guess.
 G'nite with best of love.

  Ed

SUNDAY NITE
16 DECEMBER 1945
TOKYO, JAPAN

Dear Mother –

Well, I finally got an afternoon off, today. Spent most of it walking around this neighborhood and watching the people. I never had a good chance to get around here. It was quite interesting. There sure are a lot of people around here. The one reason is that the "El" station is a block away, so they go back and forth from there. Also all sorts of shops here, such as goods, clothing, etc. I looked inside one of the food shops and couldn't figure out what 95% of the food was. It sure is different from ours. Of course, I recognized the fishheads, which they eat with rice.

The reason I got off is because my replacement is here! Yes, he arrived yesterday and will take my job when I leave next month. He's a Staff Sgt from the 106th Infantry (not Artillery) of the 27th Division. Perhaps I can relax a bit now. He shouldn't have very much trouble in picking up the work as he was a Personnel Sgt Major with the 27th Division.

Yesterday, I got two cases of American Beer. It's the last we get this month. I'm going to save some for Christmas and New Years. Well, tomorrow the 17th, will mark one year when I left home to return to Ft. Lewis. That's the longest time I've ever been away from home.

Today received your letter of 3 December, yet I received yours of the 5th, several days ago. So you did get the Japanese flag alright. You probably did tell me but I haven't got the letter as yet, as it must have gone to the 164th. Yes, I know the caricature of me didn't look like me, but if you'll look up the word "caricature" in the dictionary you'll find that it means "burlesque", "grossly exaggerated". If it had been a "sketch" of me then it would have looked like me   Also received today letters from Adeline & Pauline Cary, and a Christmas Card from the O'Hara kids, with a shapshot of them, in the snow. You sure weren't exaggerating when you said that Sharon is getting to be a lovely girl. She really is!

Well, that'll be all for this time, with the best of love,

Ed

P.S. Also enclosing a new type of yen they're printing now.

Monday
2030
17 December 1945
TOKYO, JAPAN

Dear Mother —
    I have just finished working here at the office, the reason being that men with 55 points are leaving tomorrow for the States. Also men with three, or more children. So I had to get all records ready. Next time that I work on such records my name will be on the special orders. I haven't been to the movies in over a month, one reason they didn't have anything worthwhile. Tonite they're having (or had) "Of Human Bondage" with Paul Henried. I was planning to go to see it but it's too late now. However, I do intend to go Wednesday nite when they're having Charles Laughton in "Captain Kidd". I really do want to see that one. Laughton is always good in any picture.
    Received today your letter of 8 December. I don't have it with me down here and can't exactly remember just what you said in it, but I'll look at it before I seal this letter up. I was really rushing around today, even though my replacement is here, however, I should be able to relax pretty soon. Hope so any way.
    Some of the men who are leaving for the States, didn't come into the Army until March of this year and didn't come overseas until August!! They have three children that's why they're going. Here I've been in for almost four years.
    Well, a week from tomorrow is Christmas, but it sure doesn't feel like it, especially with the rain we're having today. Also I haven't heard any radio for over three weeks so haven't heard any Christmas carols.
    Well, that'll be all for tonight with best of love,

Ed

Tuesday
1830
18 Dec. 45
TOKYO

Dear Mother –

Well, the 55-point men left for Stateside this morning. Some of them were my men from Co. "M" and many of them came over to tell me "goodbye" which made me feel pretty good, 'cause they had remembered me.

Now, the next group which leave will have me in it! At least, this time I won't have to worry about it being too hot on the ship.

There's some more about Buffalo in today's paper, and am enclosing a clipping of it. I guess there's no place like Buffalo when it comes to snowstorms.

Things are getting a little better settled here at Hq and I hope they'll continue doing so.

Well, I reckon that's about all for December 18th, with best of love –

Ed

Thursday
2020
20 Dec. 45
TOKYO

Dear Mother –

Well, I heard about the good news from the 8th Army today –
the point score from January 1st, will be 50 points or 42 months (3 ½
years) service. I have <u>both,</u> <u>53</u> points and <u>47</u> months service. It hasn't
been in the paper as yet but the 8th Army called up and asked for names
of all men who will be eligible as of 1 January.

Well, Buffalo really is getting a lot of snow according to
the papers here. Am enclosing clipping from yesterday's and today's
paper. You'll notice about the heatwave in Australia. They have the
same climate as in the States, only it's turned <u>around</u>! Right now their
summer is beginning. When we, in the States, suffer from the heat
during July, they have snow. Of course, you've probably known this
from your school days.

I saw a good move last nite. It was "Captain Kidd", a pirate
picture, with Charles Laughton.

Really has been cold but still no snow here in Tokyo. The
winter here doesn't really begin till January.

I've sent out the phonograph record to you. I'll probably be
home before it arrives. Hope it arrives safely. I packed in newspapers and
between plywood. There are two sides, one for you and the other for the
O'Hara kids. By the way the name on the record is "Ohira", name of the
music company I guess.

Well, g'nite for now, with best of love –

Ed

Thursday Evening
2040
20 December 1945
TOKYO, JAPAN

Dear Mother:

Not very much news today but thought I'd send a few lines if only to say "hello". Well, I've moved into my new quarters and it's not too bad. We've put in a couple of stoves and also I have my new radio. Anyway, in the Army it's pretty easy to get used to new surroundings. Even if not very comfortable, especially after 4 years in the Army.

The weather warmed up a bit today and it's raining outside now.

Well, the day is drawing near when I'll be leaving here and going to the 4th Replacement Depot, near Yokohama. That's the place where all troops are processed, uniforms checked to see that they're ok, etc. There the soldier stays at least two days, but sometimes as long as two weeks, before the water transportation is available. I haven't been doing very much lately as my successor has been doing most of the work. I'm driving over to Yokohama tomorrow again, to go to the 8th Army. If I get a chance I'll check up to see if I can get any further dope as to when we'll be leaving. Out of 1,120 men in this battalion, only 79 of us are eligible to leave as of January 1st.

Well, I guess that'll be about all for tonite. Goodnite with best of love,

Ed

Thursday
2010

3 January 1946

Tokyo, Japan

Dear Mother:

After not receiving any mail for several days I got 11 of them today, including yours of 23 and 24 December, enclosing snapshots which I took in PI (with the monkey) and those here in Japan. Thanks a lot. They sure came out well. Please keep all those negatives aside as I want to have some more developed when I get home this month (or next). Yes, I'm still on needles and pins, waiting for a call from Hq 8th Army saying that we can start on that long ride to the U.S.

Yes, I received a Christmas Card from Rum, in which he mentioned that he and Betty were engaged.

Yes, those snapshots which I sent you were taken with my camera, but had them developed here by a Jap and he didn't do as good a job as back home. That's why I'm holding on to the 4 rolls of film, which I have, and I'll have them developed in the States.

Well, I guess that's about all for now. Any day now I'll send you a short note, saying "don't write anymore, am coming home".

Goodnight for now with best of love,

Ed

VETERANS NADJMINSITRATION REGIONAL OFFICE
151 W. Mohawk St.
Buffalo 1, N.Y.

In reply refer to: CMR #1

Mr. Edward F. Bartz
Name BARTZ, Edward F.
119-56 Long St.
C-No. 8031 828
Jamaica, LI, N.Y.

Dear Sir;

This is to notify you that the complete records pertaining to your claim are being forwarded to the Veterans Administration,

Regional Office
252 Seventh Ave.
New York, N.Y.

Accordingly, any future communications relative to your claim should be addressed to that office, and should in all instances contain your full name, and C-Number as shown above.

Very truly yours,

Date of transfer
of Case File June 28, 1946
W.A. BIRMINGHAM, Actg Manager
Form 3164b

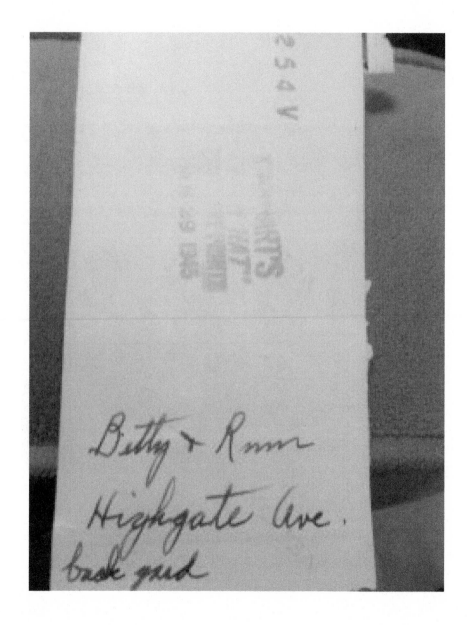

Edward Bartz with his American Legion friends.

Award given to Edward Bartz from his American Legion Post.

Roman Bartz   Edward Bartz
                   Adeline Bartz O'Hara

Picture taken for Edward's 90th Birthday!

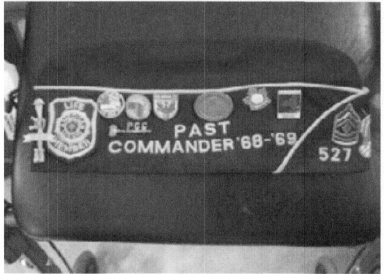

Edward's hat he wears today.

Afterward: Edward

Ed returned home from the war, and in 1946 married Corinne McGrath, a woman he had met in Massena NY when both were working for the Corps of Engineers. During the war, Corinne was stationed in Oak Ridge Tennessee, and was involved in the Manhattan Project. In 1947, the couple was living in Hempstead Long Island, New York, where Ed was working at Mitchel Air Force Base. Moving to Levittown, Long Island, they began their family in 1948 with the birth of their first child. Ed continued working for the US government at various sites: at Griffis Air Base in Rome NY, at Sunmount Veterans' Hospital in Tupper Lake, and finally at the VA Hospital in Buffalo NY. Two other children were born to Ed and Corinne during the 50s. Ed retired in 1979 after 39 years of service to the US government, but was never idle in retirement; he was a Commander of the American Legion, the President, for 27 years of the local chapter of the National Active and Retired Federal Employees, a life member of the VFW, and a lector for 30 years in his parish church. Ed for many years continued to march in the Veterans' Day parades, and visit the graves of deceased soldiers in Hamburg, New York.

Ed's mother Josephine died in 1990, at the age of 98. He lost his wife Corinne in 1996. Adeline, his baby sister, died in 2006, and Roman, his "kid brother" died in 2010. Ed lived to enjoy his 100th birthday and celebrate with a party attended by family, including his three children and his two grandchildren, as well as with long-time friends.

Afterward: Roman

Roman Bartz lived a long and productive life after World War II. He married Betty Galbreath in May 1946, and the following April they had a little girl, Cheryl. In 1956 there was another addition to the family, a son Philip. In 1976, Cheryl gave him a grandson, Dylan. In 1989, Philip and his wife LeeAnn had a baby girl Katie, and so he had a grand-daughter too.

After World War II he lived in Western New York and worked for the U.S. Army Corps of Engineers. He always loved sports, especially football and horse racing. His daughter Cheryl became a teacher in New York City. Philip became a lawyer in Washington, D.C. Roman divorced in 1980, and retired in 1985.

In retirement he thrived. He became particularly close to his son's family, and he spent much time with them in Buffalo, Washington and on vacation. LeeAnn became a second daughter to him, he doted on Katie who called him "Guppy", a nickname that stuck until the end of his life. He absolutely loved the family dog, a big yellow Labrador Retriever named Jake. They were buddies – Jake adored Roman and the feeling was fully reciprocated.

Roman lived until 91 years old, and passed after a relatively short illness in 2010. When Philip and LeeAnn told him of his serious illness, he said "I'm not too worried about it, I've lived a good long life. Now can we go get a cheeseburger and milk shake?"

His family was with him at the end. A simple obituary was written about him in the Buffalo News, and it explained his life well:

A true gentleman. A loving father and beloved grandfather. A lover of horses and dogs. A man who served his country when it needed him the most as a World War II Navy veteran. Survived by his big brother Edward Bartz, and countless other family and friends. A great man who will be missed terribly, but whose life will remain an inspiration to all of us.

It is altogether fitting that Roman Bartz is remembered in his own words in this wonderful book.

Euology for Edward Bartz
written by his daughter, Melanie Anchukaitis

Tom Brokaw's book The Greatest Generation cites this reason for the greatness of the people who came of age in the 1920s and 30s: that is, that these men and women, who fought and worked hard in every way, not for fame and recognition, but rather because it was the right thing to do. . Character was the measure of a man of this generation. And our dad, Edward Bartz, was a man of character. He was a man of integrity and a man of faith.

Our dad was never one to shy away from what was the right thing to do, no matter how challenging that might be. He went to work at the age of 16, to help support his mother, brother and sister, working in an icehouse while he finished high school. I can remember that when I was 10 or so, my father, who worked a full and tiring day as a personnel officer at the VA hospital, would come home, eat a quick dinner (because we all ate together always) and would head to the WT Grant store to work for another 3-4 hours several times a week. Yet he and my mom always made sure that we were well dressed, well-fed, and well-loved

Dad lived a life that was glorious in its scope: he was born on the eve of the first world war, was a child in the roaring twenties, came of age in the Great Depression, served his country in WWII, lived the American dream with his first home in Levittown, and his brand new 1948 Chevrolet, witnessed the assassination of a beloved president, the landing of a man on the moon, and became a part of the electronic age with his IPad .

How to live a long, productive, and happy life – the chapter page from the book of our father – or the Top Eleven Ways to a Life Well Lived.

1.Pray always –even when he did his eye drops, he would recite all of the military sites at which he had been stationed and then an Our Father, a Hail Mary and a Glory BE – model for his children….. 29 years a lector in this church with a voice so resonant and booming.

2. Love nature and care for it.—He was a gardener for years, and taught us how to plant radishes and carrots and zinnias so that we would have the satisfaction of watching them grow. He was intent on saving the wolves – a misunderstood breed, said he. (The SPCA visit

and spotting Amy, who really might have been a wolf. Casey–the Lake Placid visits the trip to the Cave of the winds The Whiteface Highway in 2004 – his reaction to the magnificence of the view. The Wild Center in Lake Placid- Costa Rica)

3. Take pride in your appearance and how you present yourself – shining shoes, showers every day, clothing clean and pressed. His attention to detail was astounding. (Grandson Jeff and the polished shoes for work)

4.Keep your mind sharp…read! (David Baldacci could not write books fast enough to feed my father's appetite for a good mystery) - keep your mind sharp – never too old to learn! (Spanish lessons before Costa Rica at the age of 83–crossword puzzles, kept a journal and balanced his checkbook to the penny)

5. Love and honor your country –perhaps because he was a first generation American, or perhaps because this greatest generation, as Tom Brokaw wrote, knew it was the right thing to do. Veterans' Day was a big deal in our home. Official visits to the funeral homes for the moving ceremony that we witnessed last evening were part of his life. He always flew an American flag, and proudly wore his WWII cap.

6.Honor your mother (visits to Nana -the letters that led to the book by Nancy Fuentes, Two Brothers, One War)

7. Love your family and teach your children well and take pride in their abilities and accomplishments - this extended to grandchildren (Eddie's law school, Rosemary's success in the business world, Kevin's PhD, Jeff's gvt. service, my teaching awards). My dad and mom always taught us to reach for the stars, to be the best, to never hide our light under a bushel basket, but rather to put it on a stand for all to see. My dad never saw limitations of gender-as well as dolls I had a train set when I was a little girl, because girls could be anything they wanted. When I was studying in Spain in 1968 and 69, my dad would write such encouraging letters to me, wanting me to travel and to experience all that I could.

8. A dollar doesn't come easily – be a good steward of your money –we may have carried this one to the extreme as a child of the depression. (and yet, never forgot a birthday, always gifts at Christmas, my birthday

back to school dress continued).

9. Be responsible -give back to society those talents you possess – one of his talents was leadership - including his military duty in the South Pacific during WWII, 39 years a government worker, 27 years as a President of NARFE, 29 a lector for his parish, Past Commander and Life Member of the American Legion.

10. Laugh – (loved the PBS show, The Last of the Summer Wine. The potatoes look good grace, BCNU long before LOL. The quick wit – Joanne the oxygen level, and "I hope that I am, Joanne")

11. Have respect for those with whom you come in contact –He was a gentleman –and a gentle man – who modeled courtesy and kindness for us always so many people talked about the respect and courtesy that he extended to them–who almost never – in my lifetime, I never remember that he lost his temper or raised his voice. Even in the last month of his life, in the rehab hospital, when he deserved to be frustrated and lose his temper, he was polite, and always asked and remembered the names of the nurses and aides.

Okay –and there is a number 12 -Eat chocolate (and drink Ovaltine – Uncle Sam's candies – eat ice cream)

In the Bible, The book of James in the New Testament demonstrates to the people of Jerusalem faith in action.
What good is it, my brothers, if someone says he has faith but does not have works? Can that faith save him? If a brother or sister is poorly clothed and lacking in daily food, and one of you says to them, "Go in peace, be warmed and filled," without giving them the things needed for the body, what good is that? So also faith by itself, if it does not have works, is dead

A life well lived, a man who loved and was loved by many. Dad, your death on All Saint's Day and your burial on Election Day are the most poignant of tributes to you. May you rest in the Lord among the Saints. Love you Dad.